MATH
GAMES
for
Clever
Kids

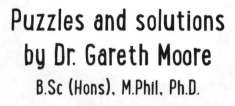

Puzzles and solutions
by Dr. Gareth Moore
B.Sc (Hons), M.Phil, Ph.D.

Illustrations and cover
artwork by Chris Dickason

☆

Edited by Jonny Marx

☆

Cover Design by Angie Allison

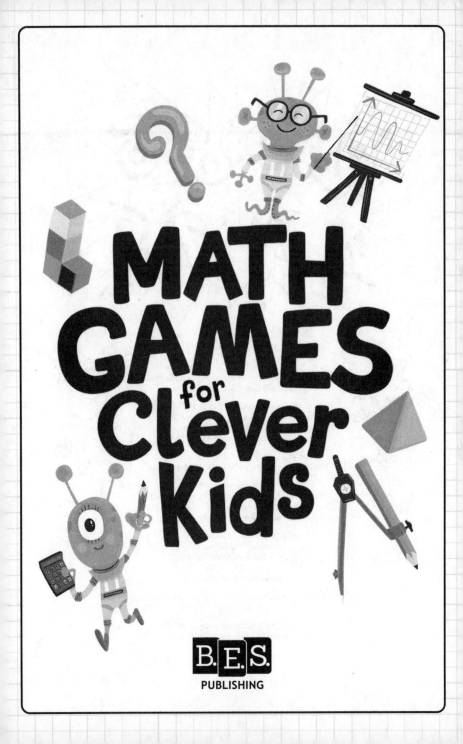

MATH GAMES
for
Clever Kids

B.E.S.
PUBLISHING

First edition for the United States and Canada published
in 2018 by B.E.S. Publishing Co.

First published in Great Britain in 2018 by
Buster Books, an imprint of Michael O'Mara
Books Limited, 9 Lion Yard,
Tremadoc Road, London SW4 7NQ

Puzzles and solutions © 2018 Gareth Moore
Illustrations and layouts © 2018 Buster Books

All inquiries should be addressed to:
Peterson's Publishing, LLC
4380 S. Syracuse Street, Suite 200
Denver, CO 80237-2624
www.petersonsbooks.com

Library of Congress Control Number: 2018940834
ISBN: 978-1-4380-1238-4

Date of Manufacture: August 2020
Manufactured by: M19A19R, Louisville (Quebec), Canada

Printed in Canada
9 8 7 6 5 4 3

INTRODUCTION

Are you ready for a challenge? This book contains 101 math puzzles that are designed to bamboozle your brain. Each conundrum can be tackled on its own, but the puzzles get steadily harder as the book progresses so you can start at the front and work your way through.

At the top of every page, there is a space for you to write how much time it took you to complete each challenge. Don't be afraid to make notes on the pages—this can be a good tactic to help you keep track of your thoughts as you work on a puzzle. There are some blank pages at the back of the book, too, which you can use for figuring out your answers.

Read the simple instructions on each page before tackling a puzzle. If you get stuck, read the instructions again in case there's something you missed. Work in pencil so you can erase things and try again.

If you're still stuck, you could also try asking an adult, although did you know that your brain is actually much more powerful than a grown-up's? When you get older, your brain will get rid of lots of information it thinks it doesn't need any more, which means you might be better at solving these games than older people are.

If you're **REALLY** stuck, have a peek at the answers at the back of the book, and then try and figure out how you could have arrived at that solution yourself.

Now, good luck and have fun!

Introducing the Math Puzzle Master:

Gareth Moore, B.Sc (Hons), M.Phil, Ph.D.

Dr. Gareth Moore is an Ace Puzzler, and author of lots of puzzle and brain-training books.

He created an online brain-training site called BrainedUp.com, and runs an online puzzle site called PuzzleMix.com. Gareth has a Ph.D. from the University of Cambridge, where he taught machines to understand spoken English.

Can you conquer the number pyramid by making sure that every block is equal to the sum of the numbers in the two blocks directly beneath it?

Here's a finished example:

For instance, 6 + 10 = 16.

Can you place the numbers 1 to 4 once each in the four empty squares so that each of the mathematical equations is correct? Two equations read left-to-right, and two read top-to-bottom.

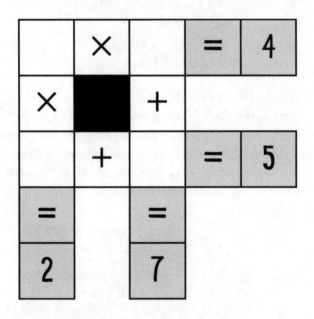

Original stack

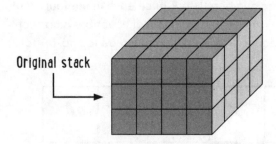

How many cubes can you count in the picture below? It started off as the 4 x 4 x 3 arrangement of cubes shown above, but someone has been stealing from the stack. None of the cubes are "floating" in the air, so if there is a cube on a layer above the bottom one, then you can be certain that all of the cubes beneath it are still there, too.

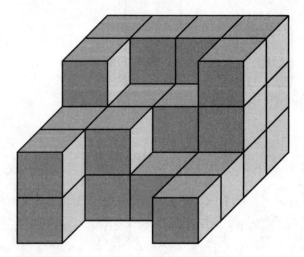

Answer: There are .... cubes.

Can you figure out which number should come next in each of these mathematical sequences?

a) 29   27   25   23   21   19   ....

b) 23   26   29   32   35   38   ....

c) 128   64   32   16   8   4   ....

d) 7   13   19   25   31   37   ....

e) 7   8   10   13   17   22   ....

Looking at these picture equations, can you figure out the value of each of the fruits?

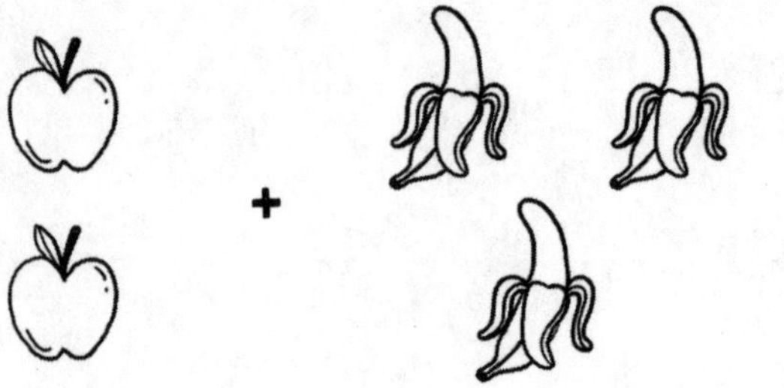

+ = 11

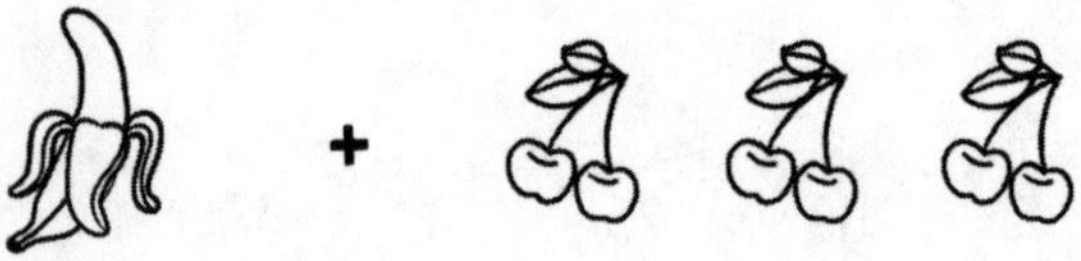

+ = 9

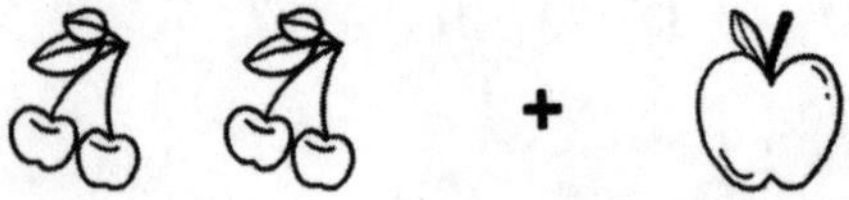

+ = 5

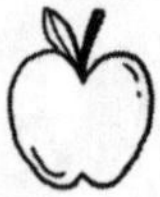

Apple 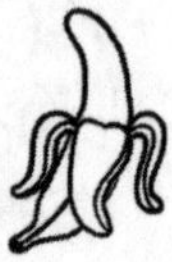 = ...   Banana = ...

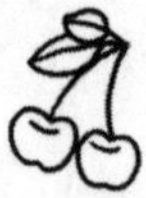

Cherry = ...

Can you use each of these mathematical operations to join a pair of numbers?

+9   **×2**   **×3**   **×5**

Pick two of the numbers below that can be joined by one of the mathematical operations above. Each number, and each operation, should be used only once. Note that there are multiple ways of joining some pairs, but only one way of doing it that allows everything to be used just once.

For example, you could use the **×5** operation to join **5** and **25**, since 5 × 5 = 25.

12	9	5
	4	13
3	25	6

Write your answers below:

....

....

....

....

....

These space monsters are marvelous at math. They have created some mental-arithmetic puzzles for you to solve.

Each of these monster chains is giving you some mathematical instructions. Begin with the number at the **START** of each sequence, and then apply each mathematical operation in turn until you reach the end of the row. Try to do all of the math in your head, without making any written notes.

Write your answer in the box at the end of each sequence.

a)

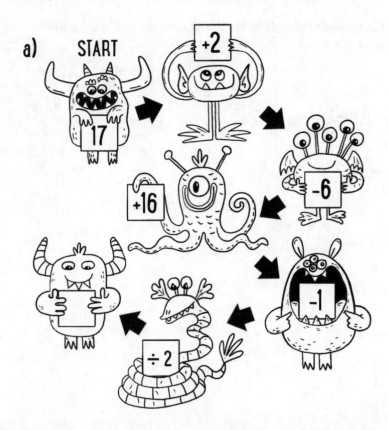

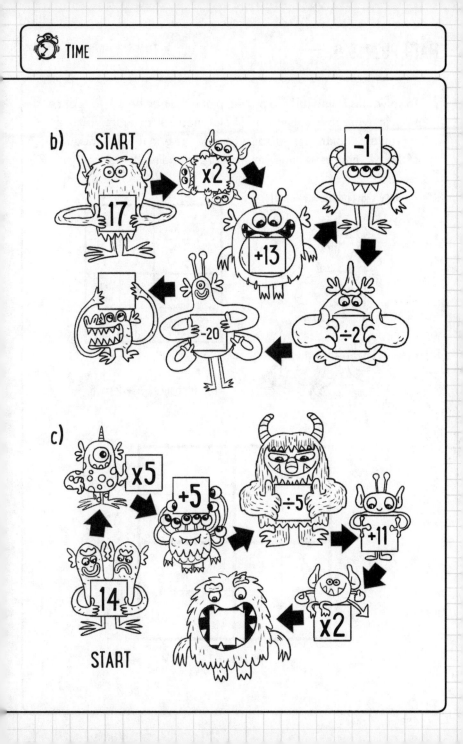

⏱ TIME ....

To solve this frame sudoku puzzle, place the numbers 1 to 4 once each in every row, column, and bold-lined 2 x 2 square, just like in regular sudoku. The numbers outside the grid tell you the sum of the two nearest numbers in the corresponding row or column.

Here's a finished example:

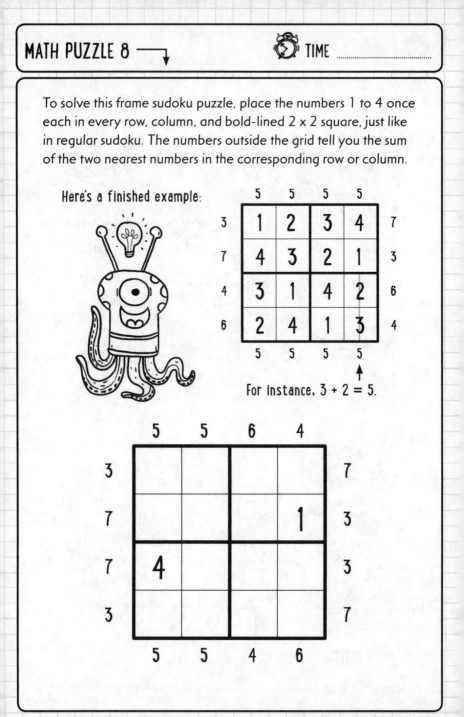

	5	5	5	5	
3	1	2	3	4	7
7	4	3	2	1	3
4	3	1	4	2	6
6	2	4	1	3	4
	5	5	5	5	

For instance, 3 + 2 = 5.

	5	5	6	4	
3					7
7				1	3
7	4				3
3					7
	5	5	4	6	

By adding together some of the numbers below, can you make each of the totals listed in the column?

4   5   7   10   11   12

You can use each number only once per total. You could form 18 by adding 7 + 11, for example, but not by adding 4 + 4 + 10.

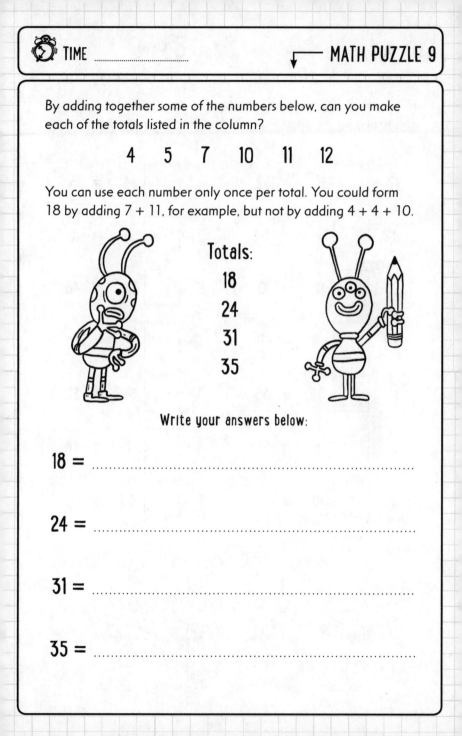

Totals:
18
24
31
35

Write your answers below:

18 = ...

24 = ...

31 = ...

35 = ...

Place a mathematical operation sign (−, ×, ÷, and +) in each empty box on the page so that every equation is correct.

12 ☐ 11 = 132   4 ☐ 4 = 16

42 ☐ 8 = 34   2 ☐ 3 = 5

120 ☐ 12 = 10   4 ☐ 12 = 48

72 ☐ 8 = 9   12 ☐ 12 = 144

17 ☐ 38 = 55   3 ☐ 10 = 30

56 ☐ 5 = 61   8 ☐ 6 = 48

32 ☐ 8 = 4   19 ☐ 43 = 62

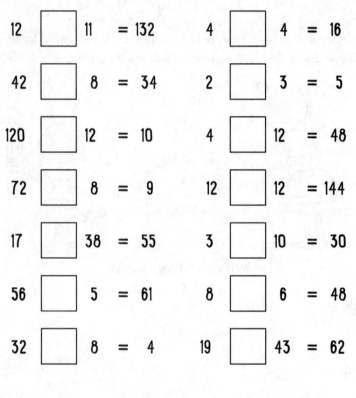

Can you form each of the given totals by choosing one number from each ring of this dartboard?

For example, you could form a total of 11 by picking 1 from the innermost ring, 8 from the middle ring, and 2 from the outermost ring. You can't pick from the same ring more than once per turn.

Totals:

12 = ...

24 = ...

26 = ...

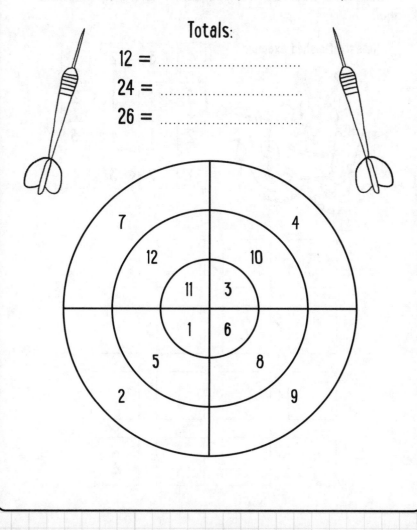

Solve this Futoshiki puzzle by placing the numbers 1 to 4 once each in every row and column. You must obey the "greater than" signs. These are arrows that always point from the bigger number to the smaller number of a pair. For example, you could have "2 > 1," or "3 > 1," or "4 > 1," since 2, 3, and 4 are greater than 1, but "1 > 2" would be wrong because 1 is not greater in value than 2.

Here's a finished example:

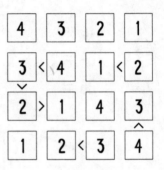

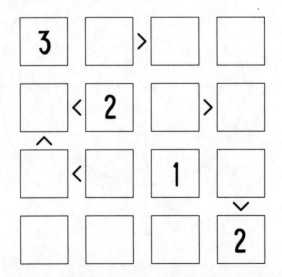

Can you complete this number-crunching maze and calculate the correct total? Begin by finding a route from the entrance at the top of the maze to the exit at the bottom. Then, add up the values on the direct route from the entrance to the exit, ignoring any dead ends you previously traveled along.

START

FINISH

Answer: The total is ....

In the distant land of Distantia they have five different values of coins, as shown below, and their currency is the cleverly named Distantian pence.

Assuming that you have as many of each value of coin as you might need, answer the following questions:

a) What is the minimum number of coins you can use to spend a total of 46 Distantian pence?

....

....

b) If you use no more than two of any value of coin, what is the maximum number of coins you can use to spend 67 Distantian pence?

....

....

c) If you buy something that costs 57 Distantian pence, what is the minimum number of coins you could receive as change from a 100 Distantian pence note?

....

....

Join multiples of 7 in increasing numerical order to reveal a hidden picture—you'll definitely know if you're correct once you've solved it!

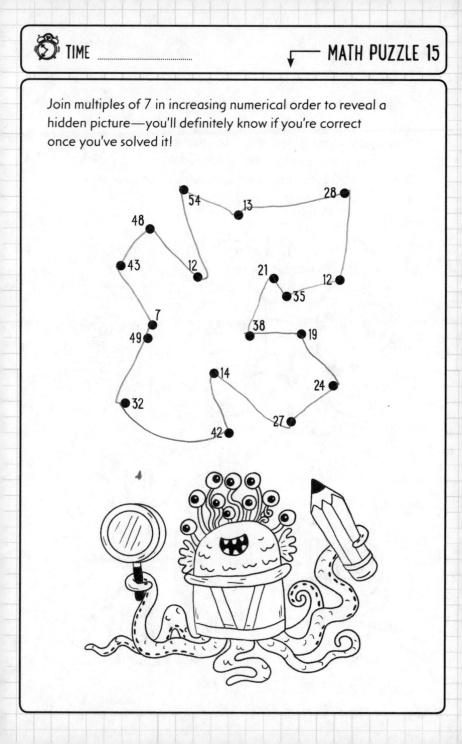

Can you figure out what is going on in these mathematical machines? In each machine, a hidden mathematical operation is taking place, converting one number to the other. For example, in puzzle **a)**, what operation could convert 4 to 12, 3 to 9, 5 to 15, and 12 to 36, as shown by the arrows? Write your answer for each puzzle in the square in the center.

a)

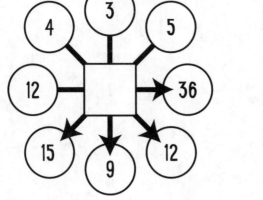

b)

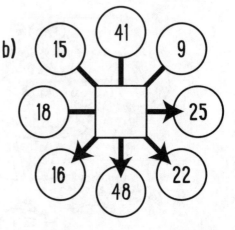

To solve this Calcudoku puzzle, place the numbers 1 to 3 once each in every row and column. You must place these numbers so that the values in each bold-lined region of grid squares add up to the small number printed in the top left-hand corner of the region.

Here's a finished example:

Numbers 1, 2, and 3 appear once in each column and each row. ⌐

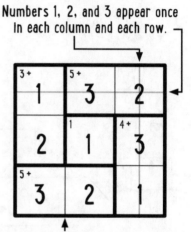

The numbers in each bold segment add up to equal the small number in the corner. For instance, 3 + 2 = 5 in this bold segment.

3+		10+
	5+	

Can you solve these perplexing pyramid puzzles by making sure that every block is equal to the sum of the numbers in the two blocks directly beneath it?

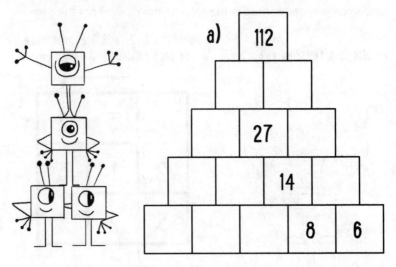

a)

112

27

14

8 6

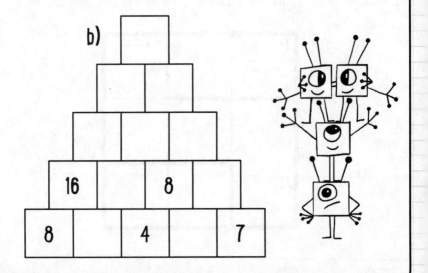

b)

16   8

8   4   7

Can you complete each of these mathematical problems by
writing the correct result in each empty box?

14 + 45 = ☐   95 - 20 = ☐

9 + 11 = ☐   28 - 20 = ☐

51 + 26 = ☐   36 + 10 = ☐

16 + 91 = ☐   10 × 6 = ☐

18 × 9 = ☐   46 - 19 = ☐

77 + 13 = ☐   77 - 28 = ☐

8 × 11 = ☐   12 × 10 = ☐

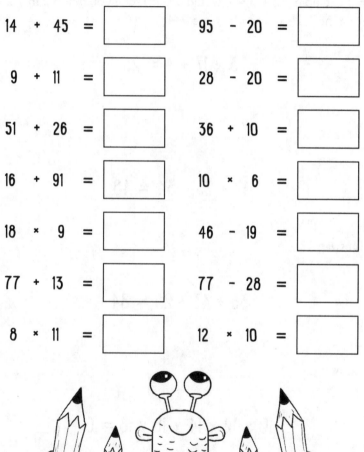

Remove exactly one digit from each of the following incorrect equations so that they become correct.

For example, 12 + 3 = 4 would be correct if you deleted the "2" from the "12" so it reads: 1 + 3 = 4.

$$3 \times 17 + 4 = 25$$

Answer: ....

$$12 + 23 + 34 = 48$$

Answer: ....

$$36 + 43 + 25 = 84$$

Answer: ....

$$10 \times 12 \times 14 \times 16 \times 18 = 0$$

Answer: ....

Can you solve each of these number anagrams? The aim is to rearrange the numbers and the mathematical operators in order to result in the given value. You can use as many brackets as you like. Remember, operations in brackets should always be completed first.

For example, given 1, 2, 3, +, and ×, you could reach a total of 9 with (1 + 2) × 3 = 9.

a)

3   4   7   +   ×

Result = 49

Answer: ....

b)

1   4   5   –   ×

Result = 15

Answer: ....

When it's 1 p.m. in the UK, it's a different time in most other countries due to the varying time zones of the world. Time zones are needed because different countries face the sun at different times, so each country's time zone is chosen so that midday in that country is fairly close to the middle of their daylight hours.

Here are four time zones:

Argentina: GMT -3 hours   **Madagascar**: GMT +3 hours

UK: GMT +0 hours   **India**: GMT +5:30 hours

So, for example, when it's midnight in the UK, it's 5:30 a.m. in India.

GMT stands for Greenwich Mean Time. It's used as a benchmark against which to measure other time zones.

Use these time zones to answer the following questions:

a) What time is it in the UK when it's 4:30 p.m. in Argentina?

....

b) When it's midday in India, what time is it in the UK?

....

c) What time is it in Madagascar when it's 8:20 p.m. in Argentina?

....

d) What time is it in India when it's 10:45 p.m. in Argentina?

....

Tick, tock . . . tick, tock . . . take a look at all of these clocks.
Can you solve the time-based questions on the opposite page?

a) How many clocks show a time that is 30 minutes past an hour?

....

b) There is one time that is shown on two different clocks. What is that time?

....

c) How many clocks can you find that show a time between 7 o'clock and 8 o'clock?

....

To solve this puzzle, draw lines along some of the gridlines in order to divide the grid up into a set of rectangles. Each number should be inside exactly one rectangle, and the sum of the width and the height of the rectangle must be equal to the value of that number.

Here's an example to show you how the puzzle works:

This rectangle, for instance, is 2 squares high by 3 squares wide, to make 2 + 3 = 5.

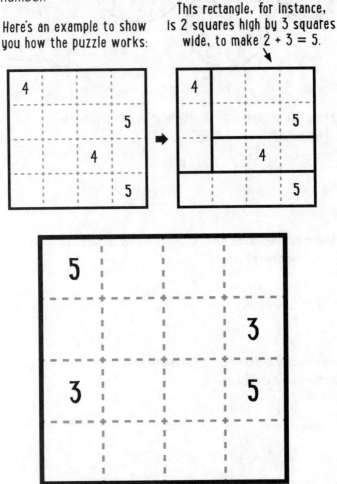

This "killer sudoku" puzzle is a variation on regular sudoku. Not only must you place the numbers 1 to 4 once each in every row, column, and bold-lined 2 x 2 square, but you must also place the numbers so that each dashed-lined region of grid squares adds up to the small number printed in the top left-hand corner of that region.

Here's an example to show you how the puzzle works:

In this dashed-lined area, for instance, 2 + 3 = 5.

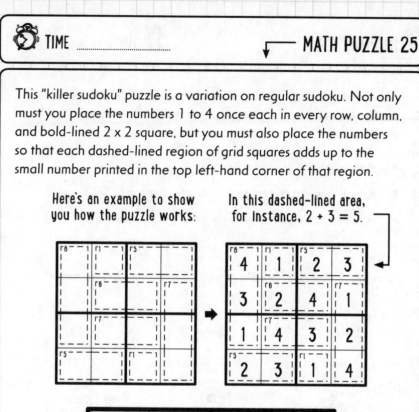

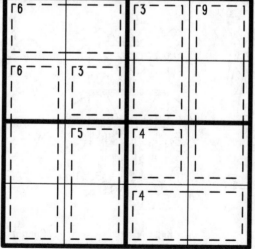

Amelia, Bella, and Connor all share the same birthday, and on their most recent birthday Connor made the following observations:

- Amelia is twice as old as I am now.

- Bella is closer in age to Amelia than I am in age to Bella.

- A year ago, Bella was twice the age I was two years ago.

- The sum of mine and Amelia's ages is 21.

Can you figure out how old Amelia, Bella, and Connor are?

Amelia　　　　　**Bella**　　　　　**Connor**

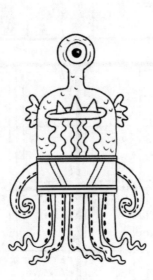

Amelia is ....　　Bella is ....　　Connor is ....

To solve this diagonal sum sudoku puzzle, place the numbers 1 to 4 once each in every row, column, and bold-lined 2 x 2 square, just like in regular sudoku. Each of the numbers outside the grid tells you the sum of the diagonal pointed to by its arrow.

Here's an example to show you how the puzzle works:

In this diagonal line, for instance, 4 + 4 + 4 = 12.

MATH PUZZLE 28 →

⏱ TIME ....

This is a kakuro puzzle. Can you place a number from 1 to 9 in each white square, so that each "run" of continuous horizontal or vertical white squares adds up to the number given to the left or the top of that "run?" You can't repeat a number within any "run," so, for example, you could form a total of 4 with 1 + 3, but not with 2 + 2.

Here's a finished example:

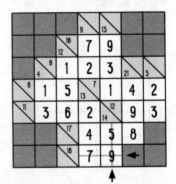

In these two "runs," for instance, 9 + 5 = 14 vertically and 7 + 9 = 16 horizontally.

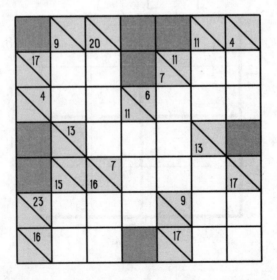

Welcome to Triangle Town, where almost everything has three sides. See how many of the following triangles you can spot and write your answers underneath. As a clue, your answers should be multiples of 3.

Scalene

Equilateral

Right-angled

....

....

....

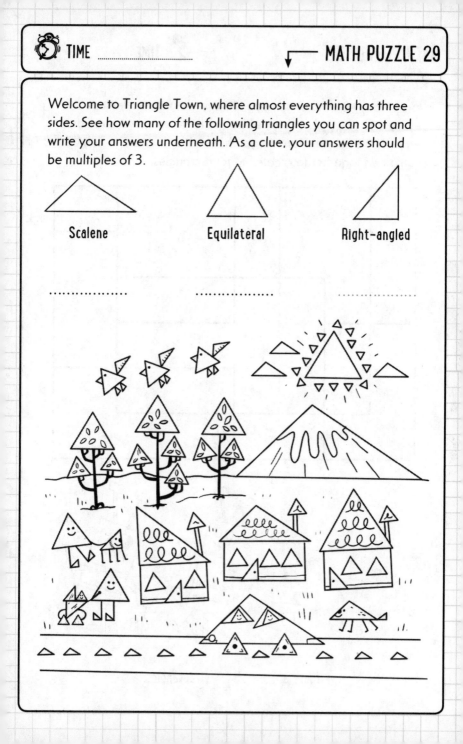

How many rectangles can you count in this image? Include every one you can find, including the large one all around the edge of the image. Don't forget that smaller rectangles can be combined together to create bigger rectangles.

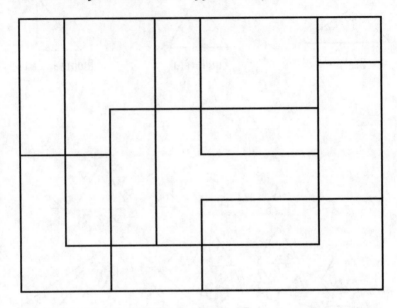

There are .... rectangles.

The following equation is incorrect, but can you **remove** just one stick in order to correct it?

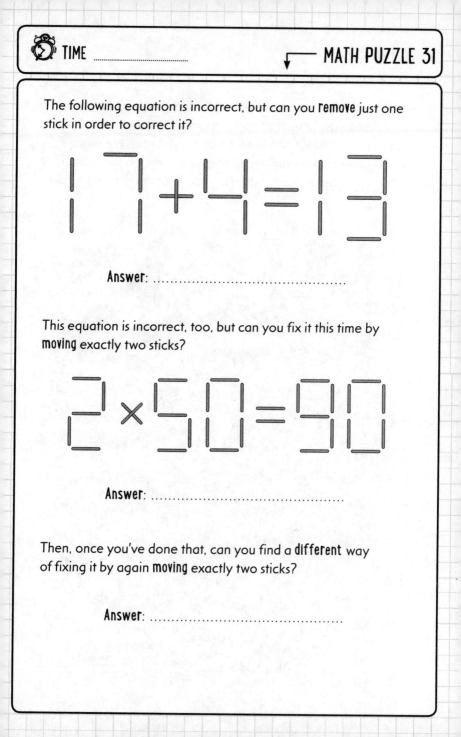

Answer: ....

This equation is incorrect, too, but can you fix it this time by **moving** exactly two sticks?

Answer: ....

Then, once you've done that, can you find a **different** way of fixing it by again **moving** exactly two sticks?

Answer: ....

Commander Callisto and Commander Comet each captain a space station and a fleet of ships separated by an asteroid belt. They share the space between the asteroids but rarely venture into opposite territories. Can you figure out the fraction-based questions on the opposite page by looking at the drawing below?

Commander Callisto   **Commander Comet**

In each of the following questions, simplify your fractions if you can. For example, 6/8 could be simplified to 3/4.

a) What fraction of all of the rockets are black?

....

b) What fraction of the white rockets are in the asteroid belt?

....

c) What fraction of the black rockets have exactly two circular windows?

....

d) What fraction of the rockets in the asteroid belt have curved fins?

....

To solve this Calcudoku puzzle, place the numbers 1 to 4 once each in every row and column. You must place these numbers so that the values in each bold-lined region of grid squares add up to the small number printed in the top left-hand corner of the region.

Here's a finished example:

Numbers 1, 2, 3, and 4 appear once in each column and each row. ⟶

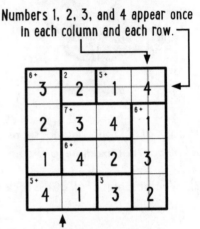

The numbers in each bold segment add up to equal the small number in the corner: 4 + 1 = 5, for instance.

1	3 +	10 +	
7+			3+
	9+	3 +	
			4

Which number is the odd one out in each of these two mathematical sets? All of the other numbers share the same property (such as, for example, all being multiples of 3), except for one.

a)

9	21	33
47	64	83

Answer: .... is the odd number out

because ....

b)

23	31	7
47	19	21

Answer: .... is the odd number out

because ....

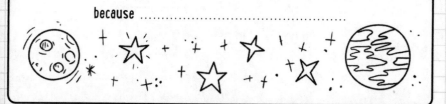

🕑 TIME ....

Can you add or subtract each of these pairs of times, and write the resulting time in the corresponding empty box? The times use the 24-hour clock, and you should add or subtract the number of hours and minutes shown to get the final resulting time.

23:25 - 04:10 = ☐

13:05 - 04:35 = ☐

06:10 + 00:40 = ☐

16:55 - 06:50 = ☐

05:45 - 03:05 = ☐

23:00 - 04:45 = ☐

13:25 - 05:45 = ☐

03:45 + 07:15 = ☐

15:35 - 03:25 = ☐

11:00 + 10:25 = ☐

Can you solve the following sums, each of which uses Roman numerals? Your answers should be in Roman numerals, too!

a) **XXX − XII =** ....

b) **XIX − V =** ....

c) **LX + XL =** ....

d) **VII + VI + V + IV + III =** ....

e) **IX × XI =** ....

f) **I + V + X + L + C =** ....

CODE

I = 1

V = 5

X = 10

L = 50

C = 100

To solve the sudoku XV puzzle on the opposite page, place the numbers 1 to 6 once each in every row, column, and bold-lined 3 x 2 box, just like in regular sudoku.

Also, wherever an "X" or a "V" joins two squares, then the sum of those two squares is either 10 (for "X") or 5 (for "V"), respectively—just like Roman numerals. If there isn't an "X" or a "V" between two squares, then those two squares definitely don't add up to either 10 or 5.

Here's an example:

		5	2		
2					4
6					2
			1	6	

The numbers here are joined by an "X," so they must add up to 10.

The numbers here are joined by a "V," so they must add up to 5.

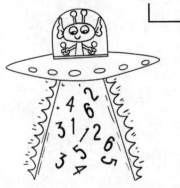

1	3	5	2	4	6
4	2	6	3	1	5
2	5	3	1	6	4
6	1	4	5	3	2
3	6	2	4	5	1
5	4	1	6	2	3

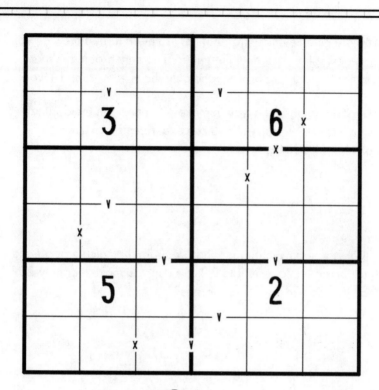

You are given a calculator that has just been turned on. Can you make it display a particular number? The only problem is that most of the keys are broken, and only the −, ×, ÷, =, and 4 work.

a) First, can you find a way to make 13 appear on the display using just 10 keypresses? You can experiment with a real calculator if you like!

Answer: ....

b) Once you have managed that, you turn the calculator off and back on again, to reset it to 0. Now can you make it display 28? Can you do it in just 10 keypresses?

Answer: ....

c) Finally, you reset the calculator to 0 again. Now can you make it display 11 in just 5 keypresses?

Answer: ....

Write a number in each empty pyramid block so that every block is equal to the sum of the numbers in the two blocks directly beneath it.

a)

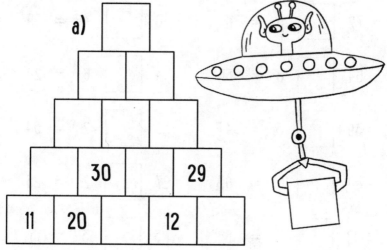

b) 244

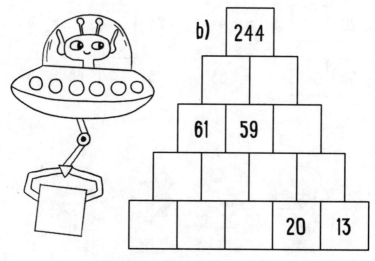

⏰ TIME ....

Place a mathematical operation sign (−, ×, ÷, and +) in each empty box on the page so that every equation is correct.

72 [ ] 6 = 12   10 [ ] 49 = 59

64 [ ] 8 = 56   4 [ ] 6 = 24

39 [ ] 8 = 47   56 [ ] 2 = 54

44 [ ] 16 = 60   27 [ ] 2 = 25

12 [−] 2 = 6   5 [ ] 3 = 15

20 [÷] 5 = 4   24 [ ] 6 = 4

58 [ ] 3 = 55   15 [ ] 68 = 83

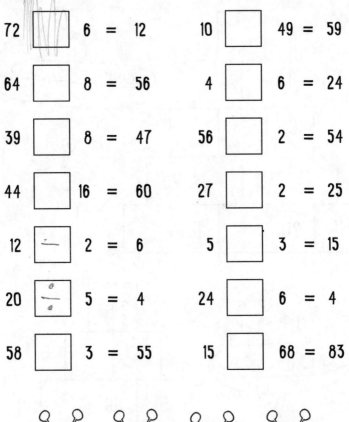

The six sides of a regular dice look like this:

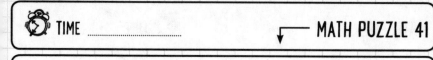

Here are five dice, all viewed from above. Unfortunately, some of the dots have rubbed off and so you can't be sure of the exact value showing on each dice:

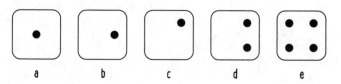

a b c d e

a) Which of the dice could be fives?

Answer: ....

b) Which of the dice could be twos? Remember that the dice faces might be rotated compared to the example faces at the top of the page.

Answer: ....

c) What is the highest possible total value of these five dice?

Answer: ....

d) What is the lowest possible total value of these five dice?

Answer: ....

Solve this Futoshiki puzzle by placing the numbers 1 to 4 once each in every row and column. You must obey the "greater than" signs. These are arrows that always point from the bigger number to the smaller number of a pair. For example, you could have "2 > 1," or "3 > 1," or "4 > 1," since 2, 3, and 4 are greater than 1, but "1 > 2" would be wrong because 1 is not greater in value than 2.

Here's a finished example:

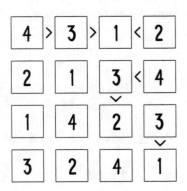

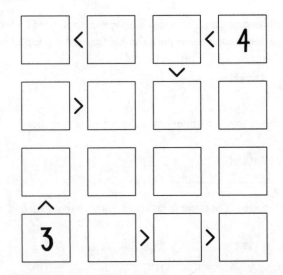

The numbers below add up to 40. By removing some numbers, you can reduce the total. For example, if you remove the 3, 6, and 11 the total is now 20.

3   5   6   7   8   11

By removing one or more of the numbers, can you make each of the totals below? Each total can be made in three different ways—can you find all three methods in each case?

29 (in 3 different ways)

1) ....

2) ....

3) ....

24 (in 3 different ways)

1) ....

2) ....

3) ....

16 (in 3 different ways)

1) ....

2) ....

3) ....

Can you form each of the given totals by choosing one number from each ring of this dartboard?

For example, you could form a total of 29 by picking 8 from the innermost ring, 10 from the middle ring, and 11 from the outermost ring. You can't pick from the same ring more than once per turn.

Totals:

32 = ...

49 = ...

53 = ...

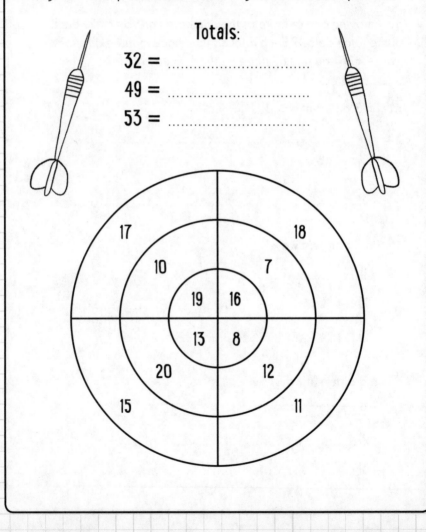

Some of the inhabitants in these skyscrapers are asleep, and some are awake. Can you answer the questions below, based on who has their lights on and who has them switched off?

a) What is the greatest number of windows you can see on a single building?

Answer: ....

b) What is the greatest number of lit rooms you can see in a single row or column of a building?

Answer: ....

Can you solve these puzzles by figuring out how many apples have been eaten?

a) Today is Friday, and each day this week I have eaten twice as many apples as I did the previous day. On Wednesday I ate eight apples. How many apples did I eat in total from Monday to Friday this week?

Answer: ....

b) I eat two apples every day, except on weekends when I only have one apple a day. In a 28-day month (starting on a Monday), how many apples do I eat?

Answer: ....

To solve this frame sudoku puzzle, place the numbers 1 to 6 once each in every row, column, and bold-lined 3 x 2 box, just like in regular sudoku. The numbers outside the grid tell you the sum of the nearest numbers in the corresponding row or column, reading up to the first bold line.

Here's a finished example:

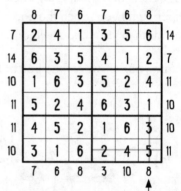

	8	7	6	7	6	8	
7	2	4	1	3	5	6	14
14	6	3	5	4	1	2	7
10	1	6	3	5	2	4	11
11	5	2	4	6	3	1	10
11	4	5	2	1	6	3	10
10	3	1	6	2	4	5	11
	7	6	8	3	10	8	

For instance, 3 + 5 = 8 vertically, and 2 + 4 + 5 = 11 horizontally.

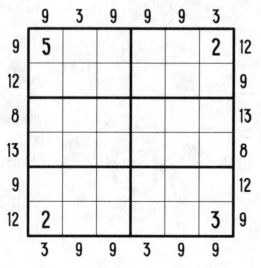

	9	3	9	9	9	3	
9	5					2	12
12							9
8							13
13							8
9							12
12	2					3	9
	3	9	9	3	9	9	

These space monsters are marvelous at math. They have created some mental-arithmetic puzzles for you to solve.

Each of these monster chains is giving you some mathematical instructions. Begin with the number at the **START** of each sequence, and then apply each mathematical operation in turn until you reach the end of the row. Try to do all of the math in your head, without making any written notes.

Write your answer in the box at the end of each sequence.

a)

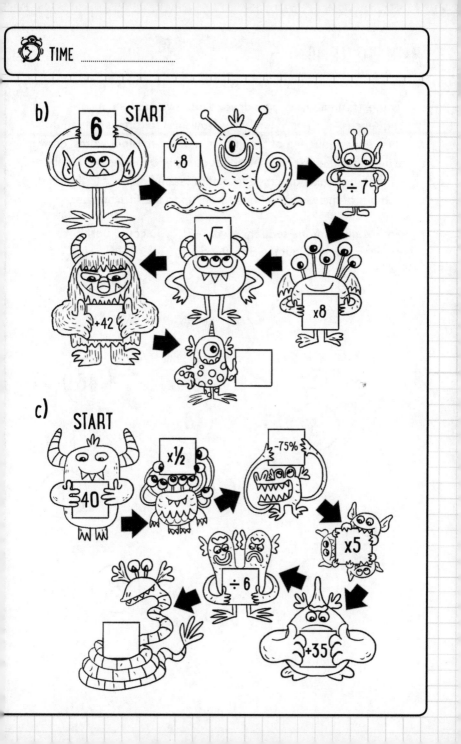

TIME

b) START
6 | +8 | ÷7 | x8 | √ | +42 |

c) START
40 | x½ | -75% | x5 | +35 | ÷6 |

These 10 numbers can be divided into two mathematical sequences, each of 5 numbers. Draw lines to form a path that joins each sequence of 5 numbers in order. In other words, draw a line from the first number of a sequence to the second number of that sequence, and then from that second number to the third number of the sequence, and so on, up to the fifth number.

For example, if one sequence was "+ 3," you could start by drawing a line to join the 3 to the 6.

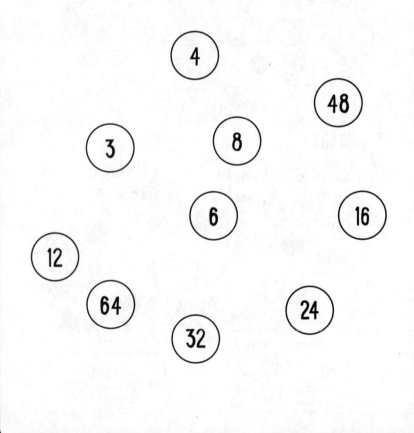

In the distant land of Yonderous they have five different values of coins, as shown below, and their currency is the cleverly named Yonderian pence.

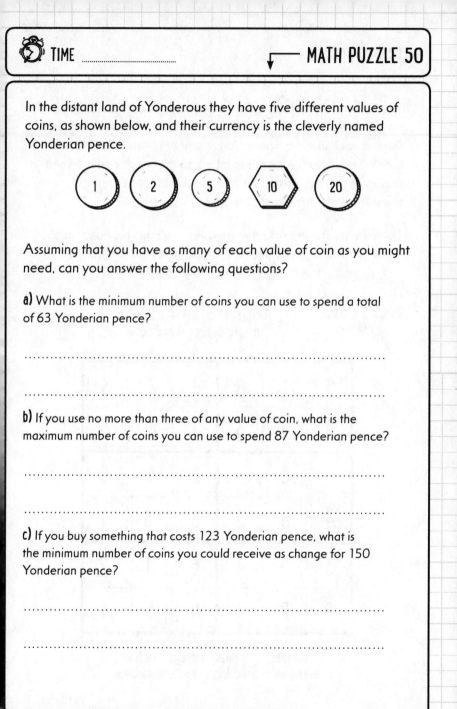

Assuming that you have as many of each value of coin as you might need, can you answer the following questions?

a) What is the minimum number of coins you can use to spend a total of 63 Yonderian pence?

....

....

b) If you use no more than three of any value of coin, what is the maximum number of coins you can use to spend 87 Yonderian pence?

....

....

c) If you buy something that costs 123 Yonderian pence, what is the minimum number of coins you could receive as change for 150 Yonderian pence?

....

....

The "killer sudoku" puzzle on the opposite page is a variation on regular sudoku. Not only must you place the numbers 1 to 6 once each in every row, column, and bold-lined 3 x 2 box, but you must also place the numbers so that each dashed-lined region of grid squares adds up to the small number printed in the top left-hand corner of that region.

There's also one important extra rule: You can't repeat a number inside a dashed-lined cage, so, for example, the solution to the "10" region in the puzzle below couldn't be 4 + 4 + 2.

Here's a finished example:

For instance, 6 + 4 + 2 = 12 in this dashed-lined cage.

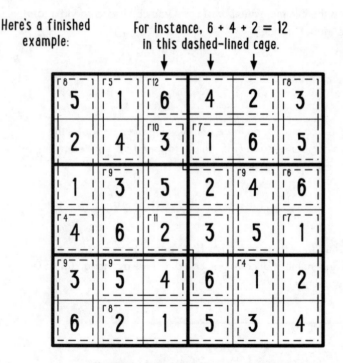

Numbers 1-6 must fit once each in every bold-lined box, row, and column.

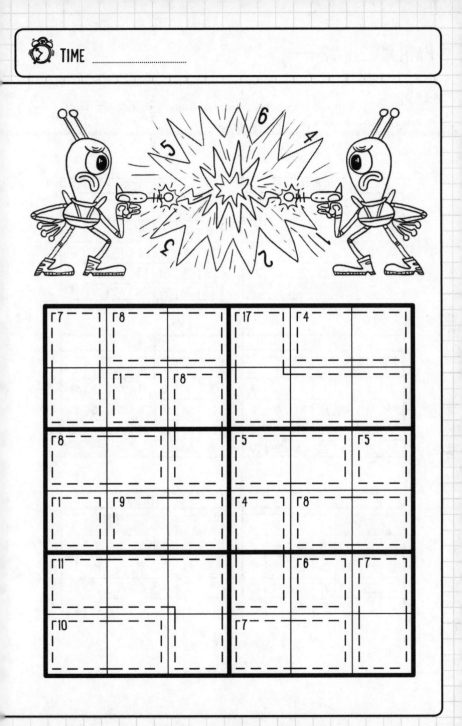

Take a look at the calendars below and see if you can answer the questions on the opposite page.

SEPTEMBER						
1	2	3	4	5	6	7
8	9	10	11	12	13	14
15	16	17	18	19	20	21
22	23	24	25	26	27	28
29	30					

OCTOBER						
		1	2	3	4	5
6	7	8	9	10	11	12
13	14	15	16	17	18	19
20	21	22	23	24	25	26
27	28	29	30	31		

NOVEMBER						
					1	2
3	4	5	6	7	8	9
10	11	12	13	14	15	16
17	18	19	20	21	22	23
24	25	26	27	28	29	30

DECEMBER						
1	2	3	4	5	6	7
8	9	10	11	12	13	14
15	16	17	18	19	20	21
22	23	24	25	26	27	28
29	30	31				

JANUARY						
			1	2	3	4
5	6	7	8	9	10	11
12	13	14	15	16	17	18
19	20	21	22	23	24	25
26	27	28	29	30	31	

FEBRUARY						
						1
2	3	4	5	6	7	8
9	10	11	12	13	14	15
16	17	18	19	20	21	22
23	24	25	26	27	28	

a) If it's September 1st today, how many days is it until October 23rd?

Answer: ....

b) If yesterday was February 4th, how many days ago was November 11th?

Answer: ....

c) If two weeks from today will be Christmas Day, how many days is it until New Year's Day?

Answer: ....

Can you place the numbers 1 to 9 once each in the nine empty squares so that each of the mathematical equations is correct? Three equations read left-to-right, and three equations read top-to-bottom.

	+		+		=	24
+	■	÷	■	×		
	×		÷		=	8
+	■	÷	■	−		
	×		−		=	9
=		=		=		
20		1		20		

Which of the three shapes, circle, square, or triangle, weighs the most? And which of the three shapes weighs the least?

In each of the pictures, assume that the distance from the pivot in the middle is irrelevant.

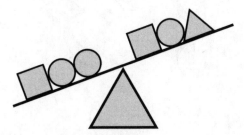

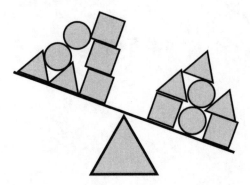

.... weighs the MOST.

.... weighs the LEAST.

Looking at these picture equations, can you figure out the value of each of the items?

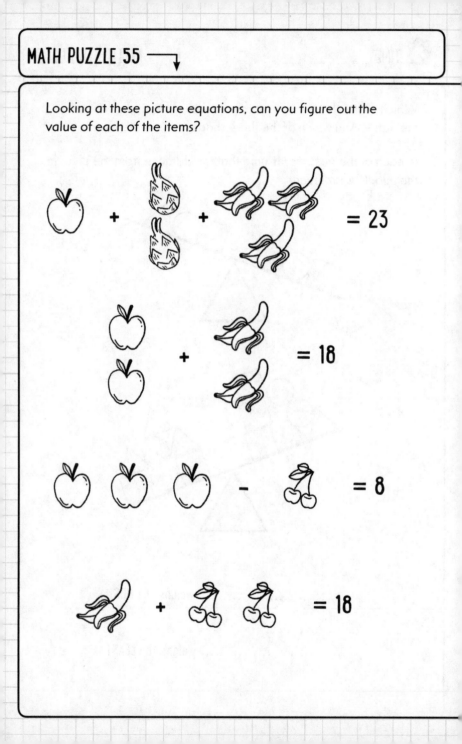

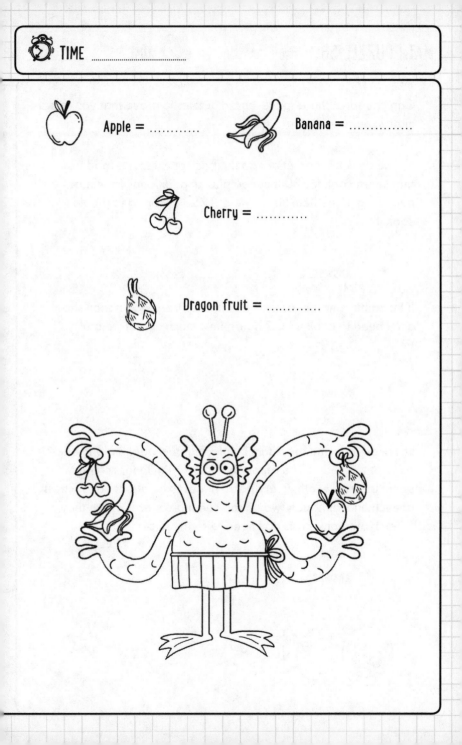

TIME ....

Can you solve these space-based puzzles to prove that you're a math supernova?

a) The cooking instructions on the back of my space food state that I must cook for 30 minutes, plus an additional 15 minutes per 250 g. If the item I have weighs 750 g, how long should I cook it?

Answer: ....

If I then buy another of the same item at the space station shop and I need to cook it for 2 hours, how much does it weigh?

Answer: ....

b) I need to fix my spaceship by placing steel panels along one edge of the vessel. The repair should be 14 m long, and each panel is 1 m in width. Every panel needs to be attached to a post at each end, although two panels can share a post where they meet. How many posts do I need to fix my ship?

Answer: ....

A regular pack of 52 playing cards contains 4 different suits (hearts, clubs, spades, diamonds), each of which contains 13 cards (Ace, 2, 3, 4, 5, 6, 7, 8, 9, 10, Jack, Queen, King).

a) If I shuffle the pack and deal a single card, what is the probability that I deal an Ace? Write your answer as a fraction.

Answer: ....

b) If I shuffle the pack and deal a single card, what is the probability that I deal a heart? Write your answer as a fraction.

Answer: ....

c) If I shuffle the pack and deal a single card, what is the probability that I deal a Jack, Queen, or King? Write your answer as a fraction.

Answer: ....

d) If I shuffle the pack and then deal two cards, what is the probability that both of them are clubs? Write your answer as a fraction.

Answer: ....

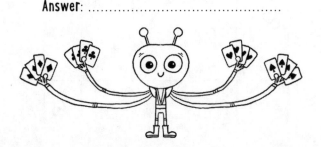

TIME ....

Solve these Futoshiki puzzles by placing the numbers 1 to 5 once each in every row and column. You must obey the "greater than" signs. These are arrows that always point from the bigger number to the smaller number of a pair. For example, you could have "2 > 1," "3 > 1," "4 > 1," or "5 > 1" since 2, 3, 4, and 5 are greater than 1, but "1 > 2" would be wrong because 1 is not greater in value than 2.

Here's a finished example:

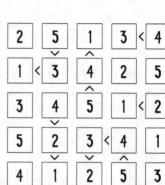

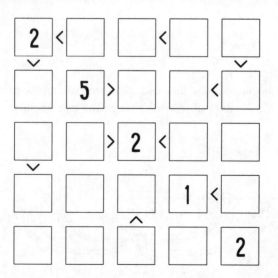

All of the questions on this page are about normal, six-sided dice.

a) What is the total value of the six sides of a dice?

Answer: ....

b) What is the maximum total value you can roll if you roll five dice?

Answer: ....

c) How many ways are there of forming a total of seven from two dice?

Answer: ....

d) What is the probability of rolling a total of seven when you roll two dice?

Answer: ....

e) What is the probability of rolling a total of ten when you roll two dice?

Answer: ....

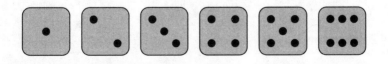

This planet is hiding all sorts of Roman numerals. Can you find all 16 of them?

Once you have found them, what is the sum of their values? Write your answer as a Roman numeral.

Answer: ....

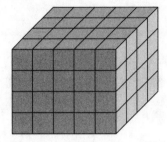

How many cubes can you count in the picture below? It started off as the 5 x 4 x 4 stack of cubes shown above, and then some were removed. None of the cubes are "floating" in the air, so if there is a cube on a layer above the bottom one, then you can be certain that all of the cubes beneath it are still there too.

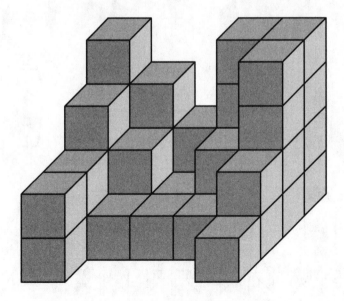

Answer: There are .... cubes.

Look at all these spaceships.

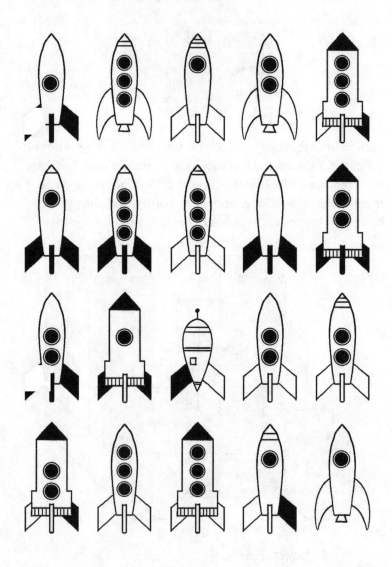

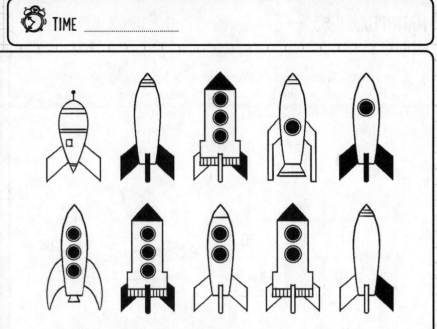

In each of the following questions, simplify your fractions if you can. For example, 6/8 could be simplified to 3/4.

a) What fraction of the rockets have two or more stripes on their nose? (The nose is the top part of the rocket.)

Answer: ....

b) What fraction of the rockets with curved fins have three windows?

Answer: ....

c) What fraction of the spaceships with an odd number of circular windows have a black nose?

Answer: ....

⏲ TIME _____

Can you conquer these number pyramids by making sure that every block above the bottom layer is equal to the sum of the numbers of the two blocks directly beneath it?

a)

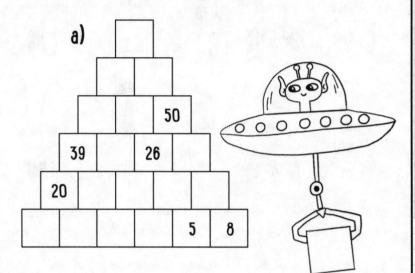

b)

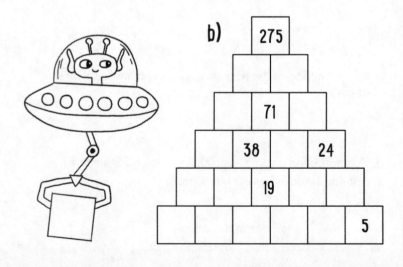

Which is the odd number out in each of these two mathematical sets? All of the other numbers share the same property (such as, for example, all being multiples of 5), except for one.

a)

27	102	75
48	56	93

Answer: .... is the odd number out

because ....

b)

16	121	81
35	25	64

Answer: .... is the odd number out

because ....

To solve the multiples sudoku puzzle on the opposite page, place the numbers 1 to 6 once each in every row, column, and bold-lined box, just like in regular sudoku.

When two touching squares are joined by a small circled number, it shows that there's a multiple bond between the connected numbers. The circle tells you how many times larger one number is than the other, so, for example, if it contains a "3" then you know that one number is three times as large as the other.

Here's an example:

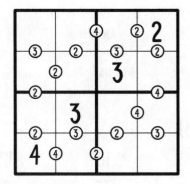

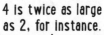

4 is twice as large as 2, for instance.

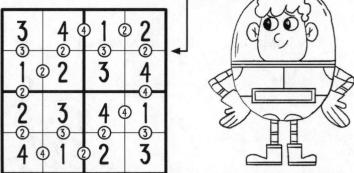

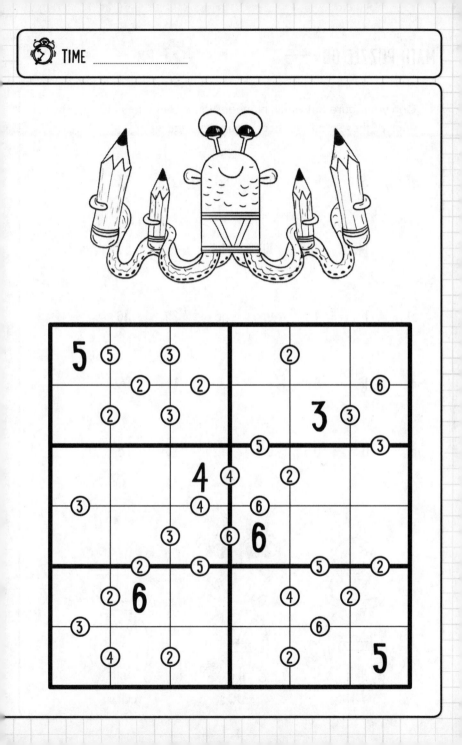

Can you figure out which number should come next in
each of these mathematical sequences, and why?

a)   3   9   15   21   27   33   ....

b)   1458   486   162   54   18   6   ....

c)   1   4   9   16   25   36   ....

d)   16   8   4   2   1   1/2   ....

e)   0.3   0.6   0.9   1.2   1.5   1.8   ....

To solve this Calcudoku puzzle, place the numbers 1 to 4 once each in every row and column. You must place these numbers so that the values in each bold-lined region of grid squares multiply to make the small number printed in the top left-hand corner of that region.

Here's a finished example:

2× 1	2	12× 3	4
6× 2	4× 1	4	3× 3
3	8× 4	2	1
12× 4	3	2× 1	2

The numbers in each bold segment multiply together to equal the small number in the corner. For instance, 4 x 3 = 12 in this bold segment.

18 ×			8 ×
	12×	2 ×	
4 ×			24 ×

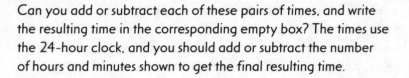

Can you add or subtract each of these pairs of times, and write the resulting time in the corresponding empty box? The times use the 24-hour clock, and you should add or subtract the number of hours and minutes shown to get the final resulting time.

22:25 − 17:25 = ☐

13:20 − 05:50 = ☐

23:55 − 12:55 = ☐

00:50 + 08:20 = ☐

09:20 + 02:20 = ☐

08:25 + 03:10 = ☐

07:55 − 04:25 = ☐

23:25 − 00:55 = ☐

18:10 − 16:50 = ☐

15:25 − 08:40 = ☐

Welcome to this quaint quadrilateral village, where almost everything has four sides. See how many of the following shapes you can spot and write your answers underneath.

Diamonds

Kites

Parallelograms

....

Squares

Trapezoids

....

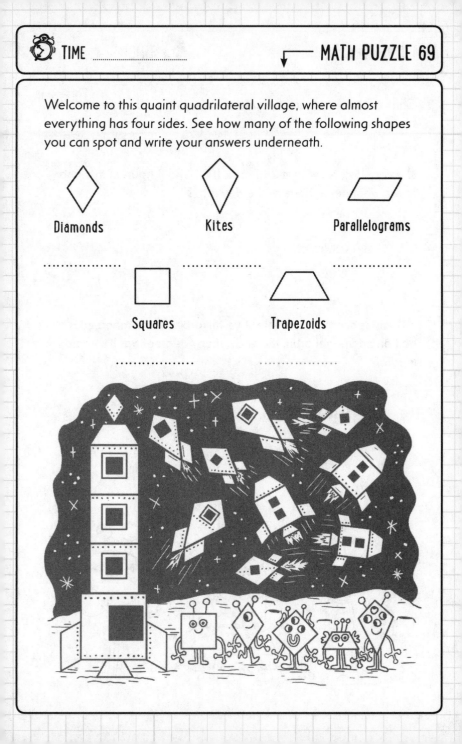

Can you complete an intergalactic mission by solving these space-based puzzles?

a) Every day consists of 24 hours. If I spend 3 hours in the lunar rover, what percentage of the day is this?

Answer: ....

b) If my spaceship completes five full orbits of the moon, plus half an additional orbit, then how many degrees has it rotated in total?

Answer: ....

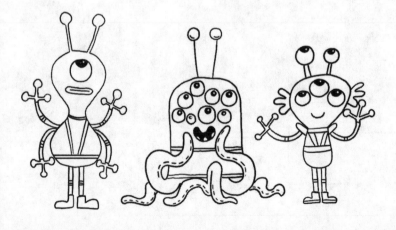

How many rectangles can you count in this image? Include every one you can find, including the large one all around the edge of the image. Don't forget that smaller rectangles can be combined together to create bigger rectangles.

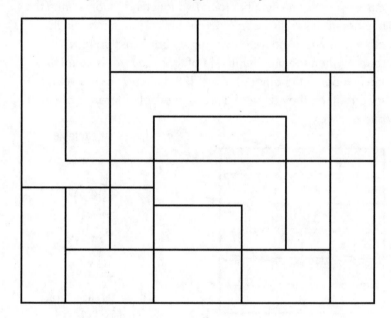

There are .... rectangles.

To solve the sudoku 1-away/2-away puzzle on the opposite page, place the numbers 1 to 6 once each in every row, column, and bold-lined 3 x 2 box, just like in regular sudoku.

Also, wherever a white bar joins two touching squares, then the number in one of those squares is equal to the number in the other plus one. And, wherever a gray bar joins two touching squares, then the number in one of those squares is equal to the number in the other plus two. If there is no bar between the squares, then they do not have a numerical difference of either one or two.

Here's an example:

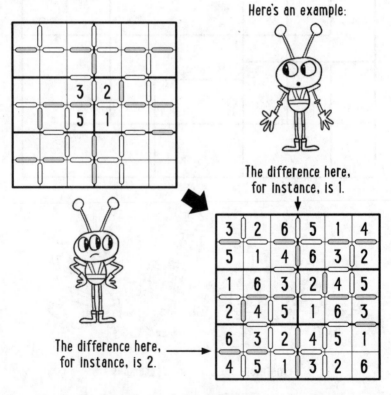

The difference here, for instance, is 1.
↓

The difference here, for instance, is 2.

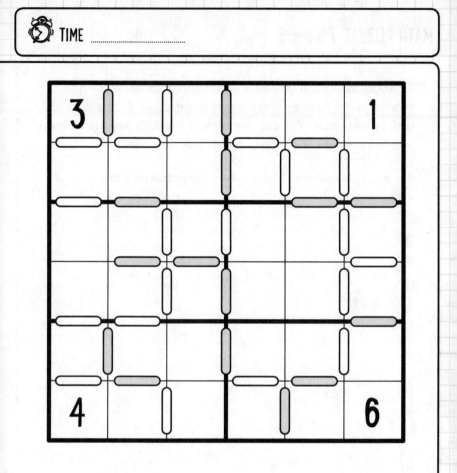

Can you solve each of these number anagrams? The aim is to rearrange the numbers and the mathematical operators to result in the given value. You can use as many brackets as you like, but you can only use each number and operator once.

For example, given 1, 2, 3, +, and ×, you could reach a total of 9 with (1 + 2) × 3 = 9.

a)

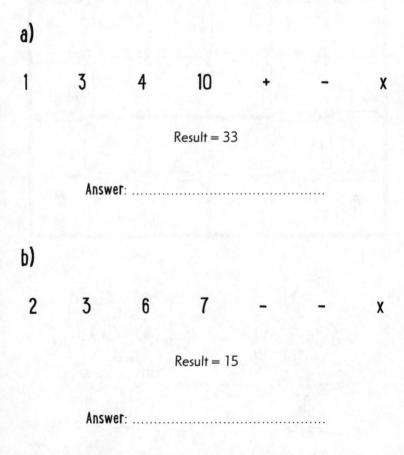

| 1 | 3 | 4 | 10 | + | − | X |

Result = 33

Answer: ....

b)

| 2 | 3 | 6 | 7 | − | − | X |

Result = 15

Answer: ....

Write a number in each empty pyramid block, so that every
block above the bottom layer is equal to the sum of the
numbers in the two blocks directly beneath it.

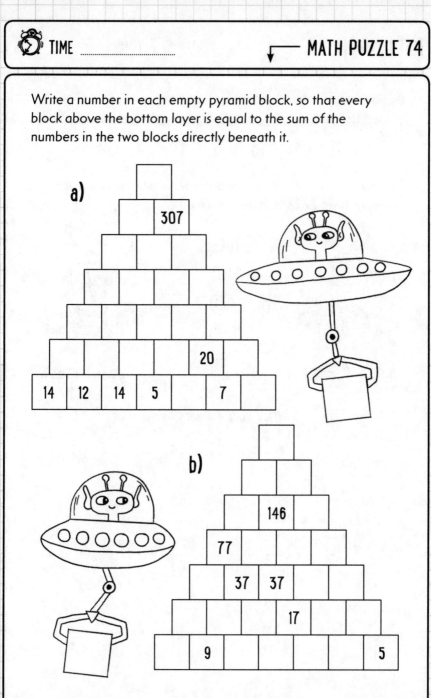

a)

307

20

14 | 12 | 14 | 5 | | 7 |

b)

146

77

37 | 37

17

9 | | | | | 5

By adding together some of these numbers, can you make each of the totals below?

11   3   18   8   17   7   4

You can use each number only once per total. You could, for example, form 27 by adding 3 + 17 + 7.

Totals:
10
20
45
60

Write your answers below:

....

....

....

....

....

....

....

Can you complete each of these mathematical equations by writing the correct numbers in each empty box?

| | ÷ 9 = 16 | 126 ÷ | = 14 |

$\boxed{} \div 9 = 16$ $\qquad$ $126 \div \boxed{} = 14$

$7 + \boxed{} = 61$ $\qquad$ $6 \times \boxed{} = 36$

$\boxed{} - 18 = 65$ $\qquad$ $2 \times \boxed{} = 16$

$95 - \boxed{} = 88$ $\qquad$ $\boxed{} \times 10 = 90$

$\boxed{} - 13 = 13$ $\qquad$ $26 + \boxed{} = 51$

$\boxed{} - 27 = 26$ $\qquad$ $50 - \boxed{} = 36$

$\boxed{} \times 4 = 12$ $\qquad$ $3 \times \boxed{} = 15$

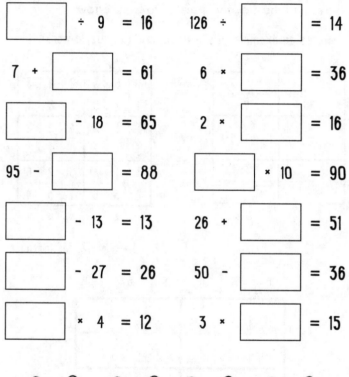

To solve this diagonal sum sudoku puzzle, place the numbers 1 to 6 once each in every row, column, and bold-lined 3 x 2 box, just like in regular sudoku. Each of the numbers outside the grid tell you the sum of the diagonal pointed to by its arrow.

Here's an example to show you how the puzzle works:

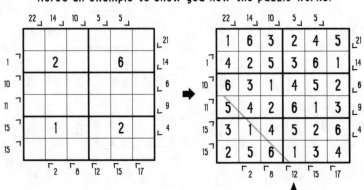

6 + 1 + 5 = 12, for instance.

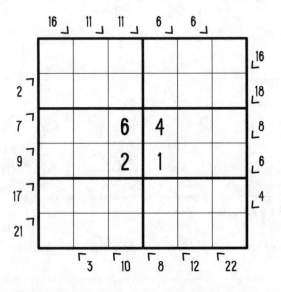

These 10 numbers can be divided into two mathematical sequences, each of 5 numbers. Draw lines to form a path that joins each sequence of 5 numbers in order. In other words, draw a line from the first number of a sequence to the second number of that sequence, and then from that second number to the third number of the sequence, and so on.

For example, if one sequence was "× 2," you could start by drawing a line to join the 3 to the 6.

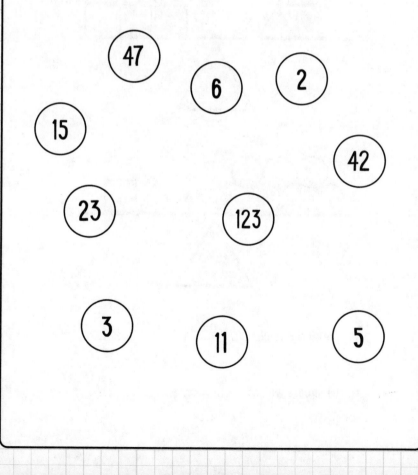

If the triangle has a weight of 11 lb (5 kg), how much do the circle and the square weigh?

In each of the pictures, assume that the distance from the pivot in the middle is irrelevant.

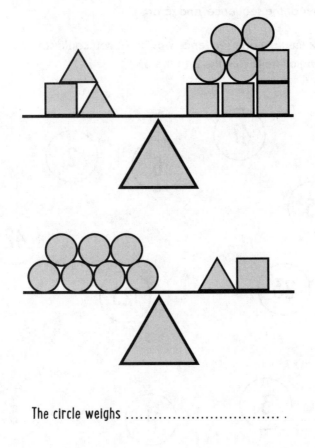

The circle weighs ....

The square weighs ....

Can you use each of the percentages at the bottom of the page to join a pair of numbers? Each number, and each percentage, should be used only once. Note that there are multiple ways of joining some pairs, but only one way of doing it that allows everything to be used once each.

For example, you could use 50% to join 32 and 64, since 32 is 50% of 64.

64   60   16

45   12   24   20

150   32   40

20% of .... is ....

25% of .... is ....

30% of .... is ....

50% of .... is ....

75% of .... is ....

Can you complete each of these monetary calculations and fill in the answers in the boxes below?

$21.60   - $1.42   =   ⬚

$2.17   - $0.76   =   ⬚

$49.40   - $43.60   =   ⬚

$32.60   - $2.40   =   ⬚

$4.83   - $1.02   =   ⬚

$4.11   + $28.90   =   ⬚

$38.90   - $29.30   =   ⬚

$1.18   - $0.28   =   ⬚

$2.97   + $4.92   =   ⬚

$23.90   - $4.94   =   ⬚

$16.50   - $0.76   =   ☐

$50   - $3.88   =   ☐

$1.74   - $1.40   =   ☐

$39.10   - $3.54   =   ☐

$2.20   + $1.69   =   ☐

$48.10   - $14.30   =   ☐

$47.60   - $0.73   =   ☐

$10.90   - $4.10   =   ☐

$38.40   - $0.07   =   ☐

$2.86   + $43   =   ☐

The "killer sudoku" puzzle on the opposite page is a variation on regular sudoku. Not only must you place the numbers 1 to 6 once each in every row, column, and bold-lined 3 x 2 box, but you must also place the numbers so that each dashed-lined region of grid squares adds up to the small number printed in the top left-hand corner of that region.

There's also one important extra rule: You can't repeat a number inside a dashed-lined cage, so, for example, the solution to the "15" region in this puzzle couldn't be 6 + 6 + 3.

Here's a finished example to show you how the puzzle works:

In this dashed-lined cage, for instance, 1 + 3 + 5 = 9.

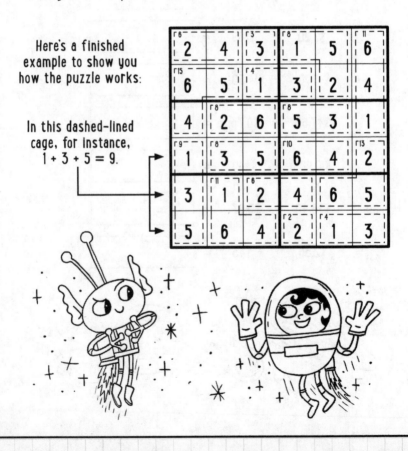

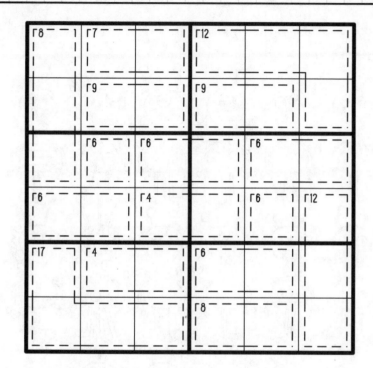

Look at all of these lovely aliens.

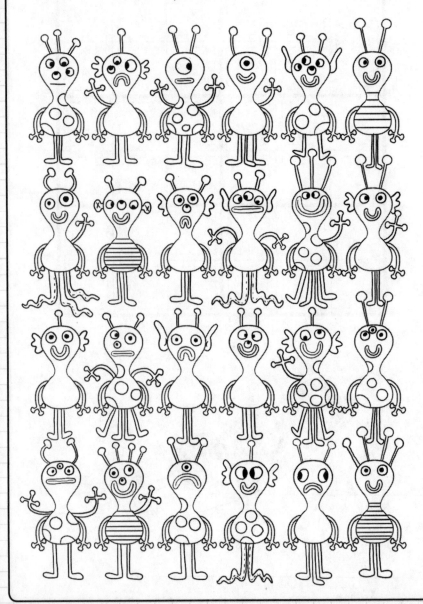

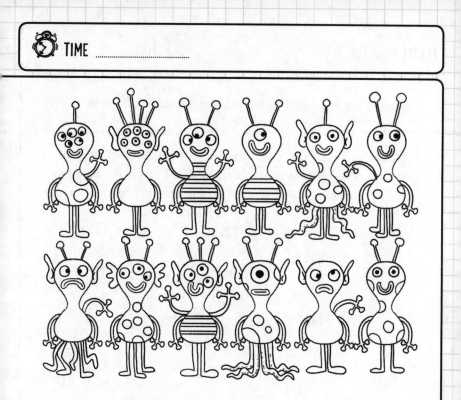

a) How many aliens have four or more eyes?

Answer: ....

b) How many of the aliens have more antennae than eyes?

Answer: ....

c) How many antennae does the alien with the greatest total number of arms, legs, and eyes have?

Answer: ....

⏱ TIME ....

Can you form each of the given totals by choosing one number from each ring of this dartboard?

For example, you could form a total of 42 by picking 13 from the innermost ring, 14 from the middle ring, and 15 from the outermost ring. You can't pick from the same ring more than once per turn.

Totals:

48 = ...
64 = ...
70 = ...

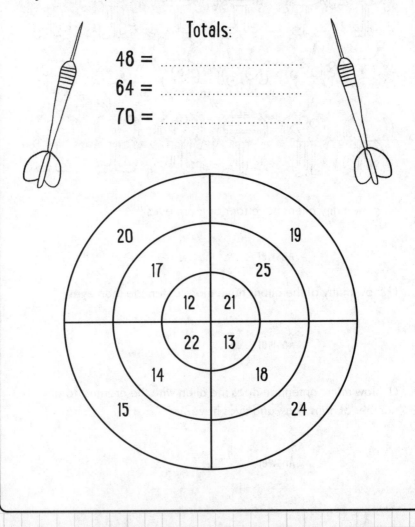

Draw lines along some of the gridlines in order to divide the grid into a set of rectangles and squares. Each number should be inside exactly one rectangle or square, and the sum of the width and the height of the rectangle or square must be equal to the value of that number.

This rectangle is 1 square high by 3 squares wide: 1 + 3 = 4.

Here's a finished example:

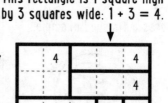

This is a kakuro puzzle. Can you place a number from 1 to 9 in each white square, so that each "run" of continuous horizontal or vertical white squares adds up to the number given to the left or the top of that "run?" You can't repeat a number within any "run," so, for example, you could form a total of 4 with 1 + 3, but not with 2 + 2.

Here's a finished example:

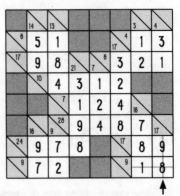

In this "run," for instance, 1 + 8 = 9 horizontally, and 8 + 9 = 17 vertically.

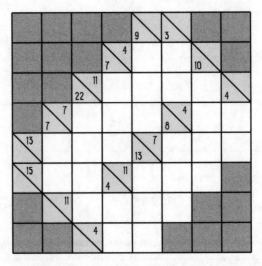

When you toss a coin you have one of two possible results:
HEADS or TAILS.

a) What is the probability of getting two heads in a row when you toss a coin twice? Write your answer as a fraction.

Answer: ....

b) And what is the probability of getting three heads in a row when you toss a coin three times? Write your answer as a fraction.

Answer: ....

c) If I toss a coin three times, what is the probability of getting two heads and one tail? Write your answer as a fraction.

Answer: ....

To solve the puzzle on the opposite page, place the numbers 1 to 5 once each in every row and column. Every place where a number is higher than the three squares touching one of its corners is marked with an arrow pointing at that corner. So, for example, the 5 in the first column of the puzzle below is greater than the square above it, the square diagonally to the right of it, and the square to the right of it.

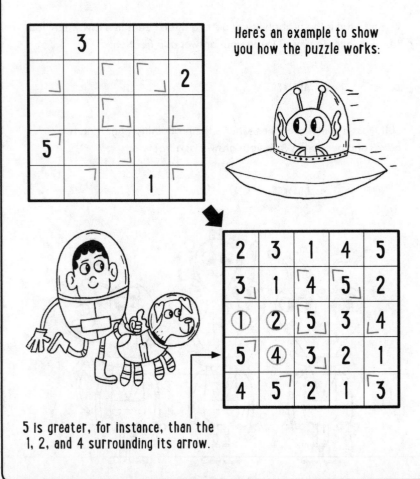

Here's an example to show you how the puzzle works:

5 is greater, for instance, than the 1, 2, and 4 surrounding its arrow.

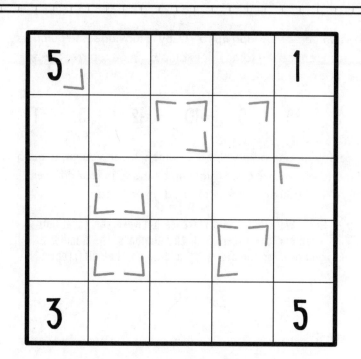

5				1
3				5

The numbers below add up to 70. By removing some numbers, you can reduce the total. For example, if you remove the 3 and 17 the total is now 50.

| 3 | 6 | 9 | 10 | 12 | 13 | 17 |

By removing one or more of the numbers, can you make each of the totals below? Each total can be made in four different ways—can you find all four methods in each case?

> HINT: Work out the difference between the total you need and the total of all the numbers. The numbers you need to remove must add up to that difference.

48

Answer 1: ....

Answer 2: ....

Answer 3: ....

Answer 4: ....

42

Answer 1: ....

Answer 2: ....

Answer 3: ....

Answer 4: ....

32

Answer 1: ....

Answer 2: ....

Answer 3: ....

Answer 4: ....

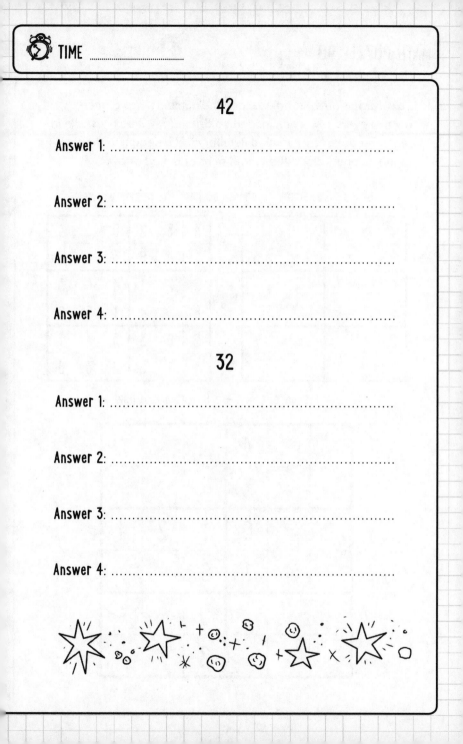

⏱ TIME ....

To solve this arrow sudoku, place the numbers 1 to 6 once each in every row, column, and bold-lined 3 x 2 box, just like in regular sudoku. Each circled number must be equal to the total of the numbers along the length of its attached arrow.

Here's an example to show you how the puzzle works:

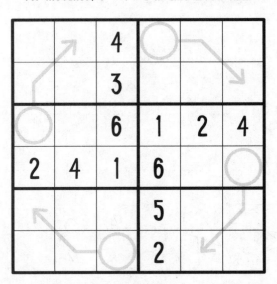

For instance, 6 = 1 + 5 in this arrow link. ⟶

Solve this Futoshiki puzzle by placing the numbers 1 to 5 once each in every row and column. You must obey the "greater than" signs. These are arrows that always point from the bigger number to the smaller number of a pair. For example, you could have "2 > 1," "3 > 1," "4 > 1," or "5 > 1" since 2, 3, 4, and 5 are greater than 1, but "1 > 2" would be wrong because 1 is not greater in value than 2.

Here's a finished example:

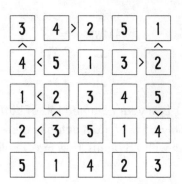

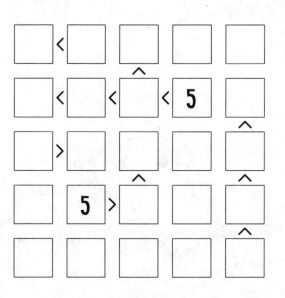

Solve these written puzzles using your marvelous math skills.

a) In my local shop, a pint of milk costs $0.55 and a loaf of bread costs $1.20. If I spend exactly $5.80, buying only pints of milk and loaves of bread, then what exactly have I bought?

Answer: ....

b) Last year I planted lots of daffodil bulbs in my garden, but only 65% of them actually grew into plants. Given that I ended up with 78 plants, how many bulbs did I plant?

Answer: ....

Which of the pictured options, a, b, or c, can replace the question mark to balance the final scale?

In all of the pictures, assume that the distance from the pivot in the middle is irrelevant.

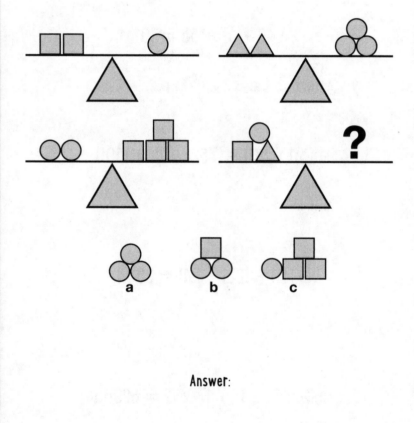

Answer:

....

Remove exactly one digit from each of the following incorrect equations so that they become correct.

For example, 12 + 3 = 4 would be correct if you deleted the "2" from the "12" so it reads: 1 + 3 = 4.

a) 46 + 37 + 58 = 101

Answer: ....

b) (30 x 50) + (75 x 90) = 1500

Answer: ....

c) 1411 + 1221 + 1311 = 2844

Answer: ....

d) 12 x 13 x 15 x 17 x 19 = 62985

Answer: ....

Can you figure out what is going on in the center box of each drawing? A hidden mathematical operation is taking place, converting one number to the other. For example, in the first picture, what operation could convert 5 to 11, and 4 to 9, and 8 to 17, and 7 to 15?

a)

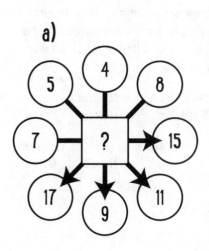

Answer:

....

Answer:

....

b)

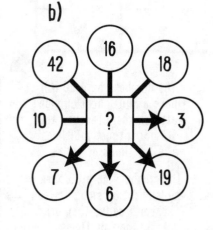

To solve the hidden multiples sudoku puzzle on the opposite page, place the numbers 1 to 6 once each in every row, column, and bold-lined box, just like in regular sudoku.

Also, every place where two touching squares contain values where one is an integer (whole number) multiple of the other is marked with a circle containing a multiplication sign between the two squares. For example, if one square contains a value that is three times the value of the other, there will be a circle on the joining line between those two squares.

Tip: A "1" will always have a circle on every side of it, so you can fill all the "1's" in right away.

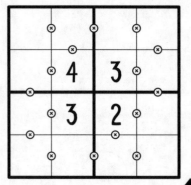

Here's an example to show you how the puzzle works:

The numbers here DO NOT have a multiplication sign between them because they are not integer multiples. 3 is 1½ times as big as 2. →

The numbers here DO have a multiplication sign between them because they are integer multiples. →

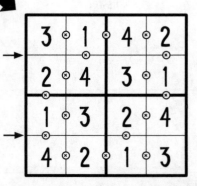

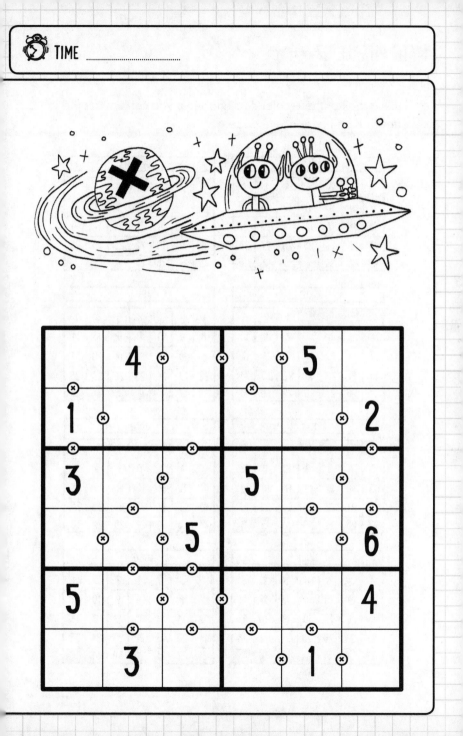

MATH PUZZLE 97

Take a look at these calendars and see if you can answer the questions on the opposite page.

JANUARY						
1	2	3	4	5	6	7
8	9	10	11	12	13	14
15	16	17	18	19	20	21
22	23	24	25	26	27	28
29	30	31				

FEBRUARY						
			1	2	3	4
5	6	7	8	9	10	11
12	13	14	15	16	17	18
19	20	21	22	23	24	25
26	27	28	29			

MARCH						
				1	2	3
4	5	6	7	8	9	10
11	12	13	14	15	16	17
18	19	20	21	22	23	24
25	26	27	28	29	30	31

APRIL						
1	2	3	4	5	6	7
8	9	10	11	12	13	14
15	16	17	18	19	20	21
22	23	24	25	26	27	28
29	30					

MAY						
		1	2	3	4	5
6	7	8	9	10	11	12
13	14	15	16	17	18	19
20	21	22	23	24	25	26
27	28	29	30	31		

JUNE						
					1	2
3	4	5	6	7	8	9
10	11	12	13	14	15	16
17	18	19	20	21	22	23
24	25	26	27	28	29	30

JULY						
1	2	3	4	5	6	7
8	9	10	11	12	13	14
15	16	17	18	19	20	21
22	23	24	25	26	27	28
29	30	31				

AUGUST						
			1	2	3	4
5	6	7	8	9	10	11
12	13	14	15	16	17	18
19	20	21	22	23	24	25
26	27	28	29	30	31	

			SEPTEMBER			
						1
2	3	4	5	6	7	8
9	10	11	12	13	14	15
16	17	18	19	20	21	22
23	24	25	26	27	28	29
30						

			OCTOBER			
	1	2	3	4	5	6
7	8	9	10	11	12	13
14	15	16	17	18	19	20
21	22	23	24	25	26	27
28	29	30	31			

			NOVEMBER			
				1	2	3
4	5	6	7	8	9	10
11	12	13	14	15	16	17
18	19	20	21	22	23	24
25	26	27	28	29	30	

			DECEMBER			
						1
2	3	4	5	6	7	8
9	10	11	12	13	14	15
16	17	18	19	20	21	22
23	24	25	26	27	28	29
30	31					

a) If it's November 3rd today, how many days is it until February 23rd of next year?

Answer: ....

b) If today was August 19th, how many days ago was April 25th?

Answer: ....

c) Tomorrow is February 29th. How many days from now is it until Christmas Day?

Answer: ....

⏱ TIME ....

You are given a calculator that has just been turned on, so it is displaying 0.

Can you make it display a particular number? The only problem is that most of the keys are broken, and only the −, ×, ÷, =, and 7 keys are working!

a) First, can you find a way to make 6 appear on the display using just 7 keypresses? You can experiment with a real calculator if you like!

Answer: ....

b) Once you have managed that, turn the calculator off and back on again, to reset it to 0. Now can you make it display 70? Can you do it in just 4 keypresses?

Answer: ....

c) Finally, reset the calculator to 0 again. Now can you make it display 100 in just 8 keypresses?

Answer: ....

Can you figure out which number should come next in each of these mathematical sequences, and why?

a)   7   17   26   34   41   47   ....

b)   59   53   47   43   41   37   ....

c)   0.15   0.3   0.6   1.2   2.4   4.8   ....

d)   35   24   13   2   -9   -20   ....

e)   3   5   8   13   21   34   ....

To solve this Calcudoku puzzle, place the numbers 1 to 4 once each in every row and column. You must place these numbers so that the values in each bold-lined region of grid squares either add up to or multiply to equal the small number printed in the top left-hand corner of that region, as indicated by either a "+" or "x" sign. Single-square regions have the value that goes in that region given directly, so you can write these straight in as soon as you begin solving.

Here's an example to show you how the puzzle works:

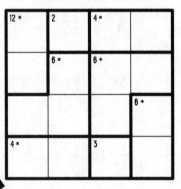

For instance, 4 x 1 = 4.

For instance, 4 + 2 = 6.

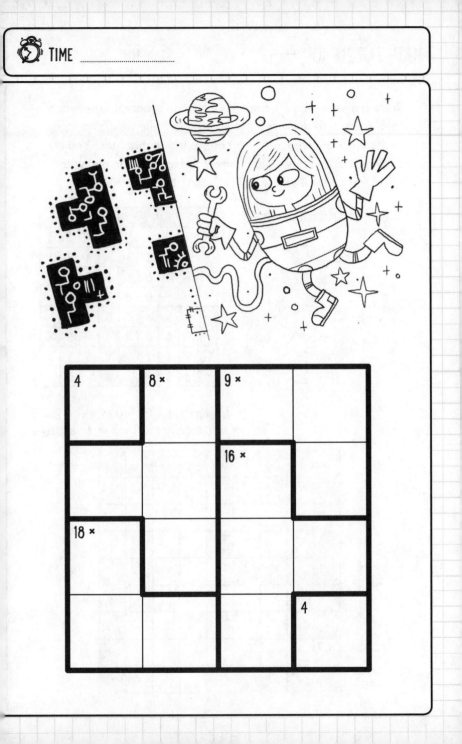

4	8 ×	9 ×	
		16 ×	
18 ×			
			4

Place a number from 1 to 9 in each white square, so that each "run" of continuous horizontal or vertical white squares adds up to the number given to the left or the top of that "run." You also can't repeat a number within any "run," so, for example, you could form a total of 4 with 1 + 3, but not with 2 + 2.

Here's a finished example:

In this "run," for instance, 1 + 2 = 3 horizontally and 1 + 3 = 4 vertically.

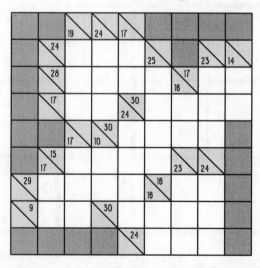

MATH PUZZLE 1

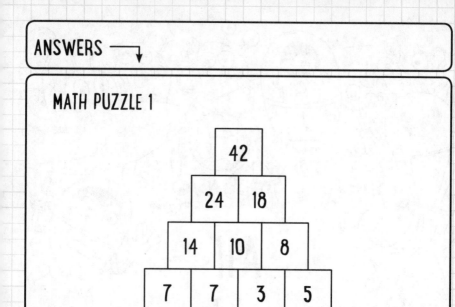

		42	
	24	18	
14	10	8	
7	7	3	5

MATH PUZZLE 2

1	×	4	=	4
×	■	+		
2	+	3	=	5
=		=		
2		7		

MATH PUZZLE 3

There are 31 cubes:

6 on the first layer (counting down from the top),
11 on the second layer, and 14 on the third layer.

MATH PUZZLE 4

a) 29   27   25   23   21   19   **17**

Subtract 2 at each step

b) 23   26   29   32   35   38   **41**

Add 3 at each step

c) 128   64   32   16   8   4   **2**

Divide by 2 at each step

d) 7   13   19   25   31   37   **43**

Add 6 at each step

e) 7   8   10   13   17   22   **28**

Add 1 in the first step, 2 in the second step, 3 in the third
step, and so on

MATH PUZZLE 5

Apple = 1   Banana = 3   Cherry = 2

MATH PUZZLE 6

$3 \times 3 = 9$ $5 \times 5 = 25$

$6 \times 2 = 12$ $4 + 9 = 13$

MATH PUZZLE 7

a) | 17 > 19 > 13 > 29 > 28 > **14** |

b) | 17 > 34 > 47 > 46 > 23 > **3** |

c) | 14 > 70 > 75 > 15 > 26 > **52** |

MATH PUZZLE 8

	5	5	6	4	
3	2	1	4	3	7
7	3	4	2	1	3
7	4	3	1	2	3
3	1	2	3	4	7
	5	5	4	6	

MATH PUZZLE 9

$18 = 7 + 11$

$24 = 5 + 7 + 12$

$31 = 4 + 5 + 10 + 12$

$35 = 5 + 7 + 11 + 12$

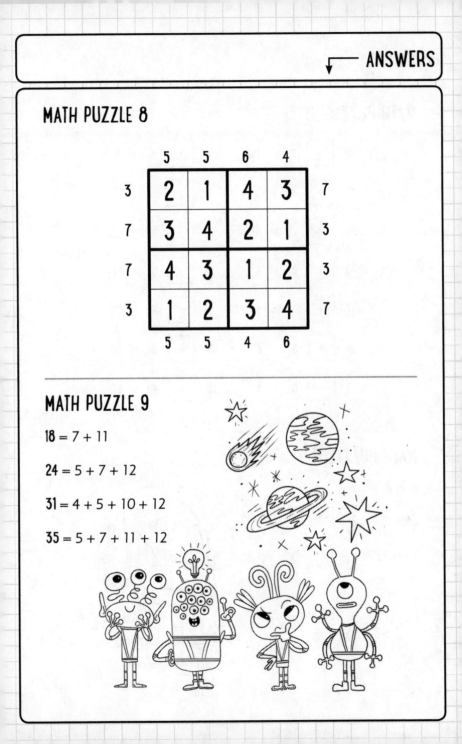

MATH PUZZLE 10

12 × 11 = 132   4 × 4 = 16

42 − 8 = 34   2 + 3 = 5

120 ÷ 12 = 10   4 × 12 = 48

72 ÷ 8 = 9   12 × 12 = 144

17 + 38 = 55   3 × 10 = 30

56 + 5 = 61   8 × 6 = 48

32 ÷ 8 = 4   19 + 43 = 62

MATH PUZZLE 11

12 = 3 + 5 + 4

24 = 3 + 12 + 9

26 = 11 + 8 + 7

MATH PUZZLE 12

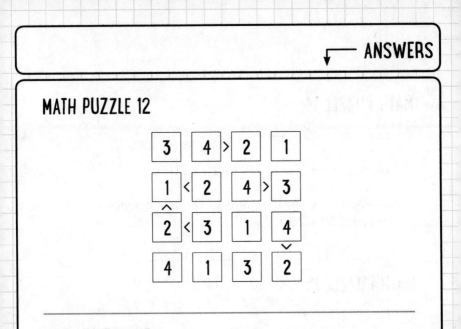

MATH PUZZLE 13

The total is 33:

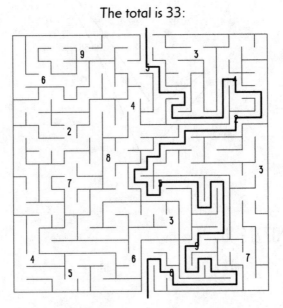

MATH PUZZLE 14

a) 4 coins: 20 + 20 + 5 + 1

b) 7 coins: 1 + 1 + 5 + 10 + 10 + 20 + 20

c) You would have change worth 43 Distantian pence, so 4 coins: 20 + 20 + 2 + 1

MATH PUZZLE 15

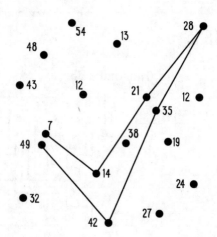

MATH PUZZLE 16

a) × 3   **b)** + 7

MATH PUZZLE 17

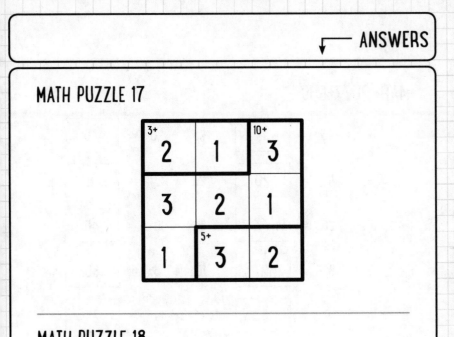

MATH PUZZLE 18

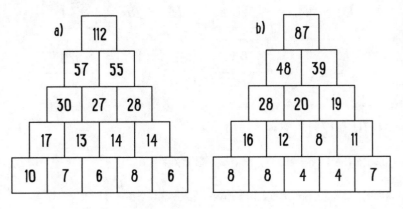

MATH PUZZLE 19

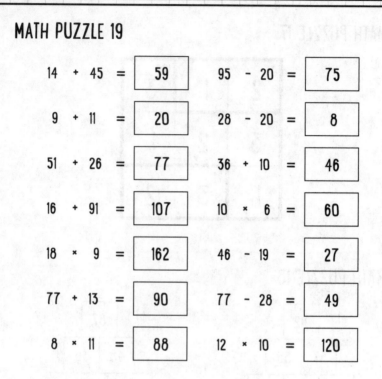

14 + 45 =	**59**	95 - 20 = **75**
9 + 11 =	**20**	28 - 20 = **8**
51 + 26 =	**77**	36 + 10 = **46**
16 + 91 =	**107**	10 × 6 = **60**
18 × 9 =	**162**	46 - 19 = **27**
77 + 13 =	**90**	77 - 28 = **49**
8 × 11 =	**88**	12 × 10 = **120**

MATH PUZZLE 20

Delete the 1 from the 17 to give: $3 \times 7 + 4 = 25$

Delete the 3 from the 23 to give: $12 + 2 + 34 = 48$

Delete the 2 from the 25 to give: $36 + 43 + 5 = 84$

Delete the 1 from the 10 to give: $0 \times 12 \times 14 \times 16 \times 18 = 0$

MATH PUZZLE 21

a) $(3 + 4) \times 7 = 49$ **b)** $(4 - 1) \times 5 = 15$

MATH PUZZLE 22

a) 7:30 p.m.   **c)** 2:20 a.m.

b) 6:30 a.m.   **d)** 7:15 a.m.

MATH PUZZLE 23

a) Two of them—5:30 on the grandfather clock, and 8:30 on the clock in the middle of the first page

b) 11:05—on the pocket watch, and on the second clock at the top of the second page

c) Two clocks—7:15 on the stopwatch, and 7:58 on the large digital clock display

MATH PUZZLE 24

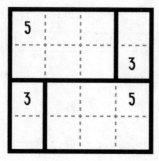

MATH PUZZLE 25

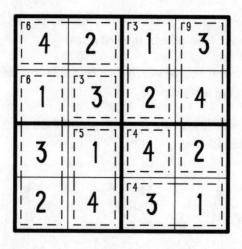

MATH PUZZLE 26

Amelia is 14, Bella is 11, and Connor is 7.

MATH PUZZLE 27

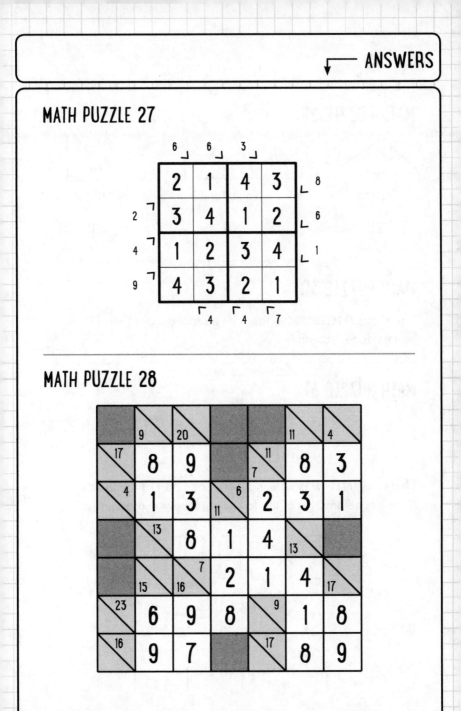

MATH PUZZLE 28

MATH PUZZLE 29

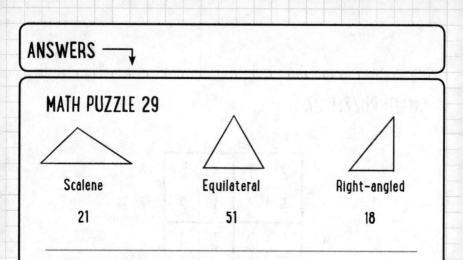

Scalene	Equilateral	Right-angled
21	51	18

MATH PUZZLE 30

There are **21 rectangles** in total. If you found more than 18, you've done incredibly well.

MATH PUZZLE 31

$$17 - 4 = 13$$

There are **three ways** of fixing the second part of the puzzle. If you found any two of the following, then you are correct:

$$2 \times 30 = 60$$

$$3 \times 30 = 90$$

$$2 \times 40 = 80$$

MATH PUZZLE 32

a) 18/40 rockets, which simplifies to 9/20

b) 7/22 rockets

c) 8/18 rockets, which simplifies to 4/9

d) 5/12 rockets

MATH PUZZLE 33

1 **1**	3+ **2**	10+ **4**	**3**
7+ **4**	**1**	**3**	3+ **2**
3	9+ **4**	3+ **2**	**1**
2	**3**	**1**	4 **4**

MATH PUZZLE 34

a): 64—all the other numbers are odd

b): 21—all the other numbers are prime numbers

MATH PUZZLE 35

23:25 − 04:10 = 19:15

13:05 − 04:35 = 08:30

06:10 + 00:40 = 06:50

16:55 − 06:50 = 10:05

05:45 − 03:05 = 02:40

23:00 − 04:45 = 18:15

13:25 − 05:45 = 07:40

03:45 + 07:15 = 11:00

15:35 − 03:25 = 12:10

11:00 + 10:25 = 21:25

MATH PUZZLE 36

a) XXX − XII = XVIII

b) XIX − V = XIV

c) LX + XL = C

d) VII + VI + V + IV + III = XXV

e) IX × XI = XCIX (Although IC is mathematically correct too, the Romans would have written it as XCIX.)

f) I + V + X + L + C = CLXVI

MATH PUZZLE 37

4	2	6	3	1	5
5	3	1	2	6	4
3	1	5	6	4	2
6	4	2	5	3	1
1	5	3	4	2	6
2	6	4	1	5	3

MATH PUZZLE 38

a) $4 \div 4 + 4 + 4 + 4 =$

$4 \div 4$ gives you 1, then add on 4 three times to result in 13.

b) $4 \times 4 + 4 + 4 + 4 =$

4×4 gives you 16, then add three lots of 4 to result in a total of 28.

c) $44 \div 4 =$

This one is a bit sneakier because you press the 4 key twice to get 44. Then you just divide by 4 to result in 11.

MATH PUZZLE 39

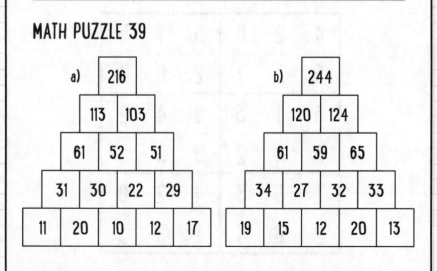

MATH PUZZLE 40

72	$\div$	6	=	12	10	$+$	49	= 59
64	$-$	8	=	56	4	$\times$	6	= 24
39	$+$	8	=	47	56	$-$	2	= 54
44	$+$	16	=	60	27	$-$	2	= 25
12	$\div$	2	=	6	5	$\times$	3	= 15
20	$\div$	5	=	4	24	$\div$	6	= 4
58	$-$	3	=	55	15	$+$	68	= 83

MATH PUZZLE 41

a) Dice a, c, d, and e could be fives.

b) Only dice c could be a two.

c) The highest possible total value is $5 + 6 + 6 + 6 + 6 = 29$.

d) The lowest possible total value is $1 + 6 + 2 + 4 + 4 = 17$.

MATH PUZZLE 42

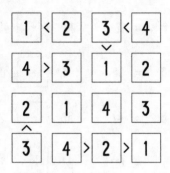

MATH PUZZLE 43

29
1) 3 + 5 + 6 + 7 + 8 (remove 11)
2) 3 + 7 + 8 + 11 (remove 5, 6)
3) 5 + 6 + 7 + 11 (remove 3, 8)

24
1) 3 + 6 + 7 + 8 (remove 5, 11)
2) 5 + 8 + 11 (remove 3, 6, 7)
3) 6 + 7 + 11 (remove 3, 5, 8)

16
1) 3 + 5 + 8 (remove 6, 7, 11)
2) 3 + 6 + 7 (remove 5, 8, 11)
3) 5 + 11 (remove 3, 6, 7, 8)

MATH PUZZLE 44

32 = 8 + 7 + 17

49 = 19 + 12 + 18

53 = 16 + 20 + 17

MATH PUZZLE 45

a) 55, on the bottom-left building. You can just count the rows (11) and columns (5) and multiply them together to get this total.

b) 8 lit windows, in the third column of the top-right building.

MATH PUZZLE 46

a) On Monday I ate 2 apples, on Tuesday 4 apples, on Wednesday 8 apples, on Thursday 16 apples, and on Friday 32 apples. This means that overall I ate **62 apples**: $2 + 4 + 8 + 16 + 32$. That's a lot of apples!

b) 48 apples: A 28-day month always has exactly 4 weeks in it, so there are 20 weekdays and 8 weekend days. That means I ate $(20 \times 2) + (8 \times 1) = 40 + 8 = 48$ apples.

MATH PUZZLE 47

	9	3	9	9	9	3	
9	5	1	3	4	6	2	12
12	4	2	6	5	3	1	9
8	3	4	1	6	2	5	13
13	6	5	2	3	1	4	8
9	1	3	5	2	4	6	12
12	2	6	4	1	5	3	9
	3	9	9	3	9	9	

MATH PUZZLE 48

a) 36 > 77 > 11 > 39 > 14 > **7**

b) 6 > 14 > 2 > 16 > 4 > **46**

c) 40 > 20 > 5 > 25 > 60 > **10**

MATH PUZZLE 49

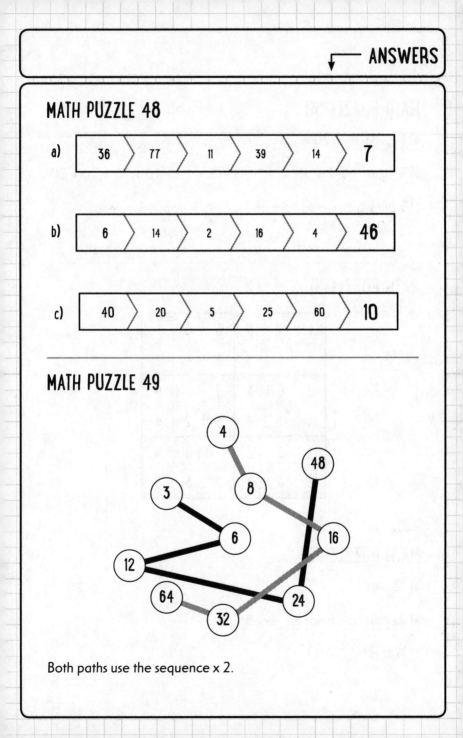

Both paths use the sequence x 2.

MATH PUZZLE 50

a) **5 coins:** 20 + 20 + 20 + 2 + 1

b) **12 coins:** 1 + 1 + 1 + 2 + 2 + 5 + 5 + 10 + 10 + 10 + 20 + 20

c) **3 coins:** You would have change of 27 Yonderian pence, so 20 + 5 + 2

MATH PUZZLE 51

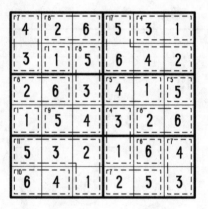

MATH PUZZLE 52

a) **52 days**

b) **86 days** (today is February 5th)

c) **21 days**

MATH PUZZLE 53

9	+	8	+	7	=	24
+	■	÷	■	×		
6	×	4	÷	3	=	8
+	■	÷	■	−		
5	×	2	−	1	=	9
=		=		=		
20		1		20		

MATH PUZZLE 54

The **circle** weighs the **MOST**.   The **square** weighs the **LEAST**.

MATH PUZZLE 55

Apple = 5   Banana = 4   Cherry = 7   Dragon fruit = 3

MATH PUZZLE 56

a) **1 hour 15 minutes**: 30 minutes + (3 x 15 minutes)

1500 g (1.5 kg)

b) I will need **15 posts** because there needs to be one on each end of the repair as well as one between each pair of steel panels

MATH PUZZLE 57

a) There are four Aces (one per suit) out of 52 cards, so the probability is 4/52 = **1/13**.

b) There are 13 hearts out of 52 cards, so the probability is 13/52 = **1/4**.

c) There are twelve of these cards (three per suit, with four suits) out of 52 cards, so the probability is 12/52 = **3/13**.

d) The probability of the first card being a club is 13/52. The probability of the next card being a club too is then 12/51. So the probability of both being a club is 13/52 × 12/51 = 1/4 × 4/17 = **1/17**.

MATH PUZZLE 58

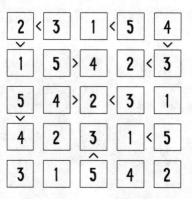

MATH PUZZLE 59

a) 21 (1 + 2 + 3 + 4 + 5 + 6)

b) 30 (5 × 6)

c) Three different ways (1 + 6, 2 + 5, 3 + 4), or six different ways if you keep track of which dice is which (1 + 6, 2 + 5, 3 + 4, 4 + 3, 5 + 2, 6 + 1).

d) 1 in 6—There are 36 different possible results for two dice, keeping track of which dice is which. So 6 out of 36 results give a total of 7, meaning the probability is 6 in 36 (1 in 6).

e) 1 in 12—There are three ways of rolling 10: 4 + 6, 5 + 5, 6 + 4, so the probability is 3 in 36 (1 in 12).

MATH PUZZLE 60

The numerals add up to **85**. This can be written as LXXXV.

MATH PUZZLE 61

39 cubes: 4 on the first layer (counting down from the top), 6 on the second layer, 12 on the third layer and 17 on the fourth layer.

MATH PUZZLE 62

a) 10/30 rockets, which simplifies to 1/3

b) 2/4 rockets, which simplifies to 1/2

c) 5/17 rockets, which cannot be simplified

MATH PUZZLE 63

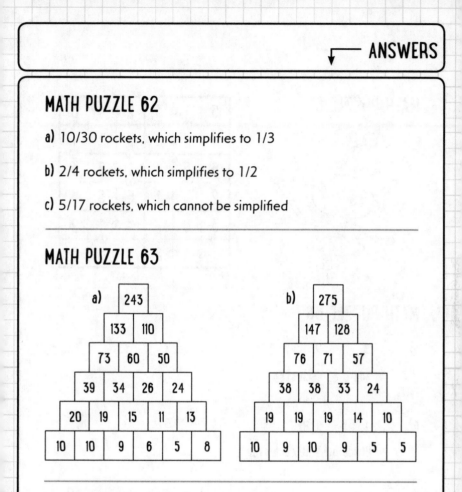

a)

243					
133	110				
73	60	50			
39	34	26	24		
20	19	15	11	13	
10	10	9	6	5	8

b)

275					
147	128				
76	71	57			
38	38	33	24		
19	19	19	14	10	
10	9	10	9	5	5

MATH PUZZLE 64

a) 56—all the other numbers are multiples of 3

b) 35—all the other numbers are square numbers (the result of multiplying a number by itself)

MATH PUZZLE 65

5 ⑤ 1 ③ 3	2 ② 4	6
4 ② 2 ③ 6	5	3 ③ 1
6	5	4 ④ 1 ② 2	3
2	3 ③ 1 ⑥ 6	5	4
3 ② 6	5	4 ④ 1 ② 2
1 ④ 4 ② 2	3 ② 6	5

MATH PUZZLE 66

a) 3   9   15   21   27   33   **39**

Add 6 at each step

b) 1458   486   162   54   18   6   **2**

Divide by 3 at each step

c) 1   4   9   16   25   36   **49**

Square numbers (or add 3, 5, 7, 9, 11, etc)

d) 16   8   4   2   1   ½   **¼**

Divide by 2 at each step

e) 0.3   0.6   0.9   1.2   1.5   1.8   **2.1**

Add 0.3 at each step

MATH PUZZLE 67

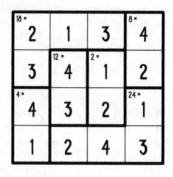

18× 2	1	3	8× 4
3	12× 4	2× 1	2
4× 4	3	2	24× 1
1	2	4	3

MATH PUZZLE 68

22:25	−	17:25	=	05:00
13:20	−	05:50	=	07:30
23:55	−	12:55	=	11:00
00:50	+	08:20	=	09:10
09:20	+	02:20	=	11:40
08:25	+	03:10	=	11:35
07:55	−	04:25	=	03:30
23:25	−	00:55	=	22:30
18:10	−	16:50	=	01:20
15:25	−	08:40	=	06:45

MATH PUZZLE 69

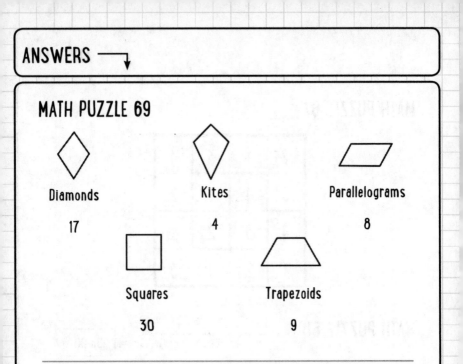

Diamonds

17

Kites

4

Parallelograms

8

Squares

30

Trapezoids

9

MATH PUZZLE 70

a) **12.5%** of the day in the lunar rover—3/24 = 0.125

b) **1980 degrees**—A full orbit is 360 degrees, so it has rotated 5.5 x 360.

MATH PUZZLE 71

There are **42 rectangles**. If you found more than 35, you've done incredibly well.

MATH PUZZLE 72

3	5	4	2	6	1
2	6	1	3	4	5
1	4	5	6	2	3
6	2	3	1	5	4
5	3	6	4	1	2
4	1	2	5	3	6

MATH PUZZLE 73

a) $(3 \times 10) + 4 - 1 = 33$

b) $(7 - 2) \times (6 - 3) = 15$

MATH PUZZLE 74

a)

643

336 | 307

179 | 157 | 150

97 | 82 | 75 | 75

52 | 45 | 37 | 38 | 37

26 | 26 | 19 | 18 | 20 | 17

14 | 12 | 14 | 5 | 13 | 7 | 10

b)

586

297 | 289

151 | 146 | 143

77 | 74 | 72 | 71

40 | 37 | 37 | 35 | 36

23 | 17 | 20 | 17 | 18 | 18

14 | 9 | 8 | 12 | 5 | 13 | 5

MATH PUZZLE 75

$10 = 3 + 7$

$20 = 3 + 17$

$45 = 3 + 7 + 17 + 18$

$60 = 3 + 4 + 7 + 11 + 17 + 18$

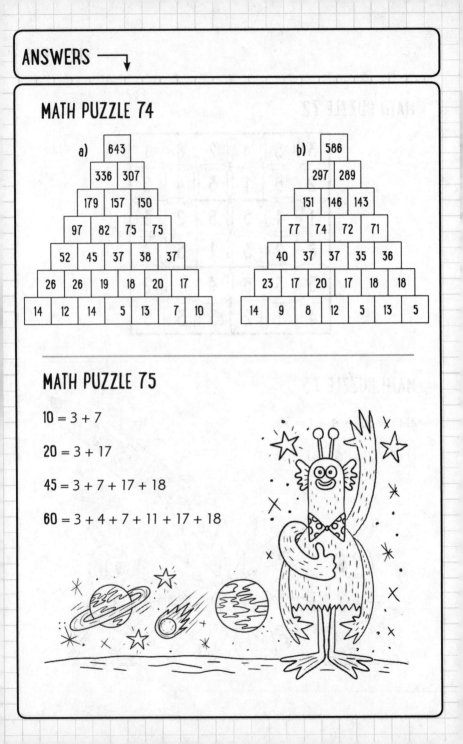

MATH PUZZLE 76

| 144 | ÷ 9 = 16 | 126 ÷ | 9 | = 14 |

7 + | 54 | = 61   6 × | 6 | = 36

| 83 | - 18 = 65   2 × | 8 | = 16

95 - | 7 | = 88 | 9 | × 10 = 90

| 26 | - 13 = 13   26 + | 25 | = 51

| 53 | - 27 = 26   50 - | 14 | = 36

| 3 | × 4 = 12   3 × | 5 | = 15

MATH PUZZLE 77

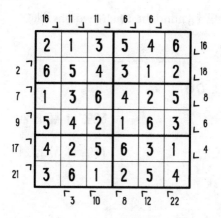

MATH PUZZLE 78

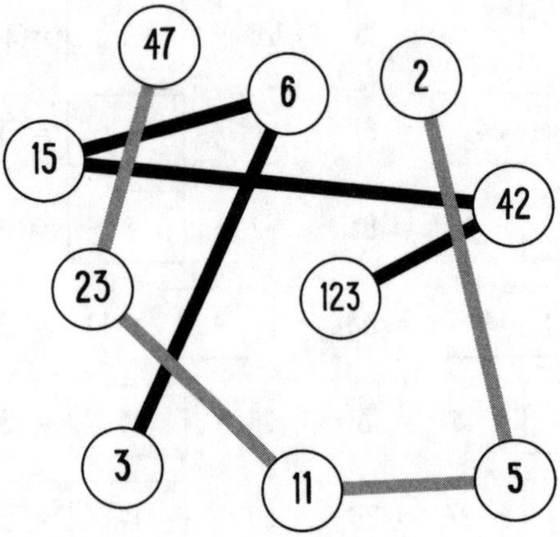

Gray line sequence: x 2 + 1

Black line sequence: x 3 − 3

MATH PUZZLE 79

The **circle** weighs **1 kg** and the **square** weighs **2 kg**.

MATH PUZZLE 80

20% of 60 is 12.

25% of 64 is 16.

30% of 150 is 45.

50% of 40 is 20.

75% of 32 is 24.

MATH PUZZLE 81

$21.60	-	$1.42	=	**$20.18**	$16.50	-	$0.76	=	**$15.74**

$21.60 - $1.42 = **$20.18** $16.50 - $0.76 = **$15.74**

$2.17 - $0.76 = **$1.41** $50 - $3.88 = **$46.12**

$49.40 - $43.60 = **$5.80** $1.74 - $1.40 = **$0.34**

$32.60 - $2.40 = **$30.20** $39.10 - $3.54 = **$35.56**

$4.83 - $1.02 = **$3.81** $2.20 + $1.69 = **$3.89**

$4.11 + $28.90 = **$33.01** $48.10 - $14.30 = **$33.80**

$38.90 - $29.30 = **$9.60** $47.60 - $0.73 = **$46.87**

$1.18 - $0.28 = **$0.90** $10.90 - $4.10 = **$6.80**

$2.97 + $4.92 = **$7.89** $38.40 - $0.07 = **$38.33**

$23.90 - $4.94 = **$18.96** $2.86 + $43 = **$45.86**

MATH PUZZLE 82

⌐8 4	⌐7 5	2	⌐12 6	1	3
1	⌐9 3	6	⌐9 4	5	2
3	⌐6 6	⌐6 5	1	⌐6 2	4
⌐6 2	4	⌐4 1	3	⌐6 6	⌐12 5
⌐17 5	⌐4 1	3	⌐6 2	4	6
6	2	4	⌐8 5	3	1

MATH PUZZLE 83

a) 4 aliens

b) 8 aliens

c) 2 antennae—it is the second alien in the third row on the left-hand page, which has a total of 11 arms, legs, and eyes.

MATH PUZZLE 84

$48 = 12 + 17 + 19$ $64 = 22 + 18 + 24$ $70 = 21 + 25 + 24$

MATH PUZZLE 85

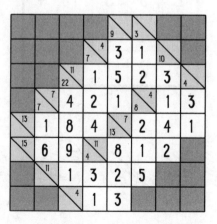

MATH PUZZLE 86

MATH PUZZLE 87

a) The probability of one head for one toss is ½. So the likelihood of this happen twice out of two tosses is $1/2 \times 1/2 = \mathbf{1/4}$.

b) The probability of three heads in succession, out of three tosses, is $1/2 \times 1/2 \times 1/2 = \mathbf{1/8}$.

c) There are three ways of getting two heads and one tail out of three tosses: head, head, tail; or head, tail, head; or tail, head, head. So there are three possibilities out of $2 \times 2 \times 2 = 8$ possible options. Therefore the probability of two heads and one tail = **3/8**.

MATH PUZZLE 88

5	3	4	2	1
4	1	5	3	2
2	5	3	1	4
1	4	2	5	3
3	2	1	4	5

MATH PUZZLE 89

48 =
3 + 6 + 9 + 13 + 17 (remove 10, 12);
3 + 6 + 10 + 12 + 17 (remove 9, 13);
6 + 12 + 13 + 17 (remove 3, 9, 10);
9 + 10 + 12 + 17 (remove 3, 6, 13)

42 =
3 + 9 + 13 + 17 (remove 6, 10, 12);
3 + 10 + 12 + 17 (remove 6, 9, 13);
6 + 9 + 10 + 17 (remove 3, 12, 13);
12 + 13 + 17 (remove 3, 6, 9, 10)

32 =
3 + 6 + 10 + 13 (remove 9, 12, 17);
3 + 12 + 17 (remove 6, 9, 10, 13);
6 + 9 + 17 (remove 3, 10, 12, 13);
9 + 10 + 13 (remove 3, 6, 12, 17)

MATH PUZZLE 90

5	2	4	3	1	6
1	6	3	4	5	2
3	5	6	1	2	4
2	4	1	6	3	5
4	3	2	5	6	1
6	1	5	2	4	3

MATH PUZZLE 91

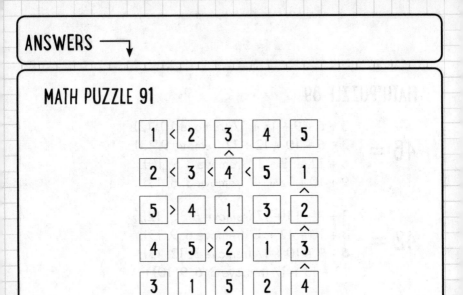

1 < 2	3	4	5
2 < 3 < 4 < 5	1
5 > 4	1	3	2
4	5 > 2	1	3
3	1	5	2	4

MATH PUZZLE 92

a) 3 loaves of bread ($3.60) and 4 pints of milk ($2.20)

b) I planted 120 bulbs

MATH PUZZLE 93

Option **a** is the correct answer.

MATH PUZZLE 94

a) Delete the 4 from the 46 to get 6 + 37 + 58 = 101

b) This is easier than it looks. You only need to spot that 3 x 5=15, and so 30 x 50= 1500. Then all you need to do is **delete the 9** from the 90 to get (30 x 50) + (75 x 0) = 1500

c) The result, 2844, ends in a 4, but the last digit of each of the three other numbers is 1, which means that the answer to the sum as printed must end in a 3. The only way to make the last digit anything other than a 1 is to **delete the final digit** of 1221 to get: 1411 + 122 + 1311 = 2844

d) The right-hand side is an odd number, so we can't have an even number on the left-hand side, since any number multiplied by an even number is always an even number too. So we have to **delete the 2** from the 12 to get 1 x 13 x 15 x 17 x 19 = 62985

MATH PUZZLE 95

a) × 2 + 1   b) ÷ 2 − 2

MATH PUZZLE 96

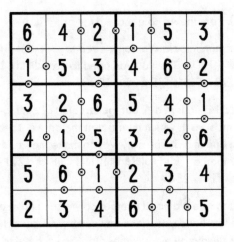

6	4	2	1	5	3
1	5	3	4	6	2
3	2	6	5	4	1
4	1	5	3	2	6
5	6	1	2	3	4
2	3	4	6	1	5

MATH PUZZLE 97

a) 112 days

b) 116 days

c) 301 days

MATH PUZZLE 98

a) $7 \times 7 - 7 \div 7 =$

7 x 7 gives you 49, from which you subtract 7 to get 42. Then you divide by 7 to result in 6.

b) $77 - 7 =$

You need to press the 7 key multiple times between calculations. Subtracting 7 from 77 results in 70.

c) $777 - 77 \div 7 =$

If you subtract 77 from 777 you get 700. Now if you divide by 7 you get 100.

MATH PUZZLE 99

a)   7   17   26   34   41   47   **52**
Add 10, 9, 8, 7, etc at each step

b)   59   53   47   43   41   37   **31**
Prime numbers in decreasing value

c)   0.15   0.3   0.6   1.2   2.4   4.8   **9.6**
Multiply by 2 at each step

d)   35   24   13   2   -9   -20   **-31**
Subtract 11 at each step

e)   3   5   8   13   21   34   **55**
Add the previous two numbers together at each step

ANSWERS →

MATH PUZZLE 100

4 **4**	8× **2**	9× **3**	**1**
1	**4**	16× **2**	**3**
18× **3**	**1**	**4**	**2**
2	**3**	**1**	4 **4**

MATH PUZZLE 101

Kakuro solution:

- Row (19/24/17 clues): 24 → 7 8 9
- 28 → 4 7 8 9 ; 25 ... 23\14 ; 17\16 → 9 8
- 17 → 8 9 ; 30\24 → 7 9 8 6
- 17\10 → 9 8 7 6
- 15\17 → 9 2 3 1 ; 23\24
- 29 → 9 7 8 5 ; 16\16 → 9 7
- 9 → 8 1 ; 30 → 7 9 6 8
- 24 → 7 8 9

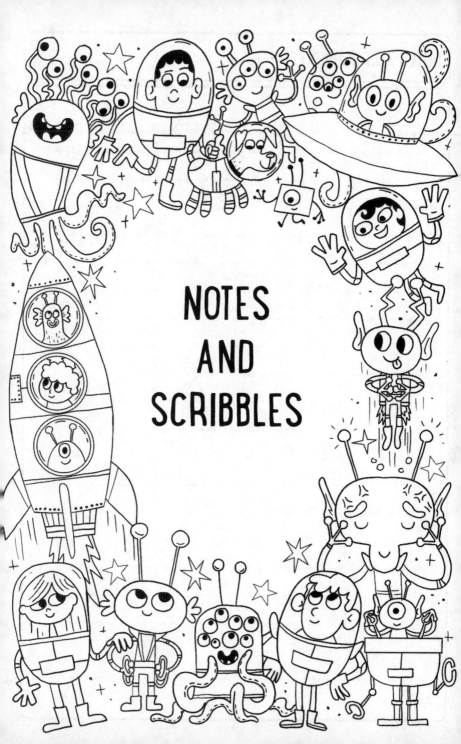

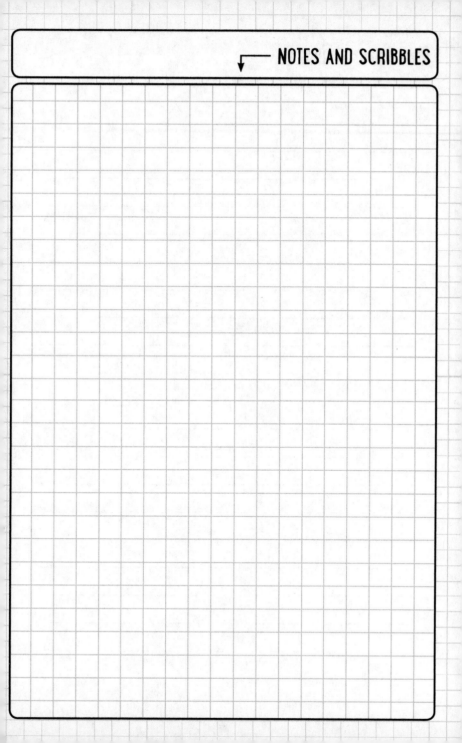

NOTES AND SCRIBBLES

NOTES AND SCRIBBLES ⟶

NOTES AND SCRIBBLES ⟶

NOTES AND SCRIBBLES ⟶

NOTES AND SCRIBBLES

NOTES AND SCRIBBLES

NOTES AND SCRIBBLES ——→